_To_ BURGUNDY _and_ BACK AGAIN

To Answer d Leon,

Thank you for supporting

the arts!

Roy Cloud

To
BURGUNDY
and
BACK AGAIN

A TALE OF WINE, FRANCE, AND BROTHERHOOD

ROY CLOUD

LYONS PRESS
Guilford, Connecticut
An imprint of Globe Pequot Press

TO DAD, WHO CAN STILL RAISE A GLASS OF
GIGONDAS WITH THE BEST OF THEM.

AND TO HELEN.

Copyright © 2011 by Roy Cloud

Lyons Press is an imprint of Globe Pequot Press.

Text design: Libby Kingsbury

Library of Congress Cataloging-in-Publication Data is available on file.

ISBN 978-0-7627-6455-6

Printed in the United States of America

10 9 8 7 6 5 4 3 2 1

Contents

Chapter 1

PROVIDENCE

I never did get to The Lido. I still haven't, although the idea tempts me wistfully every time I go to Paris. In November of 1997 I was charged with putting together a portfolio for an idealistic new wine importing company, and I went off to France to find suppliers. It was a heady and sobering time, and idle moments took on momentous weight. As I stood in line at the airport, the prospect of success or failure loomed. I was a rookie, really. I knew wine, but I had little experience with the intricacies of importing and distributing it. Then there was the fact that I spoke no French. How to navigate a culture without its language was an obstacle that plagued me from the first. But I had convinced myself that this venture was bigger than I was and that it did not warrant petty concerns. My employer counted on me, plus I had my own determination; such things evened the odds. With that reckoning, I filed into the Air France 747 amid the crowd and hubbub and found shelter in my seat.

It was the usual boarding: people hurriedly removing their coats, others pushing by with eyes on the numbered rows, and still others stuffing suitcases in the overhead compartments. Unsurprisingly, a vast number of these folks were French, and somehow distinctly looked it, too. They tended to be thin and dark, with angular features and strange clothing. I caught snippets of their conversation without understanding a word, a failure that tended to crumple my resolve, so I gave up eavesdropping to concentrate on the bulkhead movie screen. It was a three-by-four-foot screen, front and center, ten or so rows in front of me. On its white backdrop ran cinematic trailers promoting, among other things, the Paris nightclub Lido, whose chorus line of sequined dancers filled the screen and invited all viewers to consider the idea of flying to France a fabulous undertaking. I wanted to believe this, I really did. But my eyes drifted back to the French passengers, and my ears buzzed with more of their incomprehensible conversation. Then, suddenly, my mind froze as an American boy captured a two-second glimpse of a topless Lido dancer and helplessly exclaimed: "TITTIES!" Everyone, in that instant, stopped. I can still see the little lady stretching full tilt with a suitcase overhead, her eyes turned sharply at the sound; the fat man blocking an aisle, his brow furrowed deeply at what he was sure he'd just heard; the college student searching a bin for extra pillows, her face flush with amusement. As for the boy, I never was able to pinpoint him. By the time I looked, embarrassment had driven him to the deck. But he made me laugh, bless his heart, and that lifted the fear from me.

My father, who was much on my mind at the time, would have leaned over and elbowed me had he been there. He had always readily embraced amusement. I wouldn't be able to tell him about the boy, but I could tell my older brother Joe, who would meet me in Paris the very next day. He would laugh, too. He was my secret weapon, my solution to the language problem, for Joe spoke French—well, too, of course, as my older brother had succeeded at all things academic. Me, I was more hit-or-miss in that department.

The new wine company had charged me with assembling a book of growers (or the French *vignerons*, if you prefer the more exotic term—and we certainly did—referring to those small farmers who made a living tending their own vines and making their own wine). I had twelve days to accomplish the goal, which was wildly optimistic. I knew this better than anyone. It accounted for the endless preparations I made during the weeks leading up to the plane ride, and it accounted for the routing bouts of terror that came like jolts of electricity and grew in duration as the days grew shorter. But I was going to get on that plane. I was going to meet those growers. I was going to do everything I could to assemble a book of them and their wines.

Those twelve days turned into a journey that changed my life.

My first insight that wine could hold the key to other worlds came while I was in college. This happened on the back veranda of a colonial farmhouse in Hadley, Massachusetts, on one of those river-humid summer evenings (we sat overlooking the Connecticut). The house was a nonprofit historical museum, and we happened to be on that veranda because my girlfriend worked in the museum as a part-time interpreter. With us were her American history professor and his wife, both twenty-some years our senior. They were there because the professor was utterly smitten by his student, but he hadn't told his wife that, and he certainly hadn't told me.

His other passion was German wine — Mosel Riesling to be exact — and he had generously brought two Kabinett-grade bottles of the stuff. He saw that I was an interested novice, so he explained how the Mosel River meandered amid these super-steep, slate-filled hillsides laced with vineyards that rose high above little villages, whose inhabitants frequently made their living making wine, as their ancestors had, century after century. He spoke of the importance of the grower and the site, and told us that Kabinett was the first grade of wine in the highest echelon of German wine. It was wine made from the first picking, the lightest and the most delicate.

This wine was like no other that I had ever tasted. It wasn't just delicate; it was *intensely* delicate. That was what set it apart. It smelled of honeysuckle and green apples, and tasted of the very slate itself, which intrigued me immensely. The professor said, and I understood, that only from the Mosel and its tributaries could wine like this be found. I sniffed and tasted it eagerly, even raptly. At one point I took the bottles in hand to study the labels. Condensation beaded off the glass in the summer humidity, and I realized excitedly that I could peel the labels off and save them. Then it hit me that I was drunk, and I looked up. The conversation had stopped. The professor was staring hopelessly at my girlfriend; his wife was staring coldly at the three of us. They were too old, we were too young, and wine, alas even this wine, had its limitations.

But I never forgot the wine. From that day forward, I became an avid student of the libation.

The second time wine spoke singularly to me was during a Christmas while I was in graduate school in New York City. I had come home for the holiday to Berkeley, California, where my folks had relocated. Joe was there too, having flown down from Seattle where he then lived. Because we hadn't seen each other in months, Dad opened a bottle of Ridge 1984 Geyserville Zinfandel for lunch one day. The '84 was the current release, and that wine danced right out of the bottle. It could have been the brilliantly chilly West Coast afternoon, or the fact that we were all together again (and downing vino at lunch!), but whatever the reason that zesty zin struck me as one of the most delicious wines that I had ever had up to that point. With all its luscious fruit the wine proclaimed *California!* in spades.

By that Christmas, I was a completely hooked oenophile. In New York I worked at one of the city's early wine bars while doing my graduate studies. Once I finished my degree, I moved down to Washington DC to join Helen, my future wife. Here I got a job at MacArthur Liquors. This, I knew from reading wine guru Robert Parker's newsletter, was the District's top wine store. I figured I would be paid for engaging in my passion while I went about the other more important things in my life. During the course of my tenure at MacArthur's, however, wine became the more important thing.

In one sense in the 1980s and '90s, MacArthur's was just another East Coast dump of a wine store. There was none of the lovingly varnished hardwood racks displaying bottle upon bottle of fine wine, handled by gentlemen in bow ties and cardigans who enjoyed nothing more than discussing the nuances of nature's finest bounty. Instead, there was dust—endless amounts of it. The store had a beastly ventilation system that coughed dust by the horrid lungful, where it came to settle onto the bottles lying in cheap steel cage racks and onto a ratty carpet so embedded with the stuff that the little household vacuum cleaner bought to defeat it never stood a chance.

Dust, I came to understand, was a metaphor. It stood for the seedy male liquor stores that had sprung up like mushrooms after the drought of Prohibition had ended. They were seedy because liquor was a cutthroat business and there was no real money to be made retailing it; they were particularly male because liquor had long been the domain of men; and they were associated with the East because the West Coast was quicker to embrace wine as a lifestyle (that varnished wood phenomenon).

In that era, despite the dust, MacArthur's managed to occupy a loftier plane than the run-of-the-mill wine and spirits joints. The store had an owner astute enough to see that wine offered a way out of the desperate dark corridor of liquor sales, and savvy enough to do business direct with European merchants, particularly Bordeaux merchants, bypassing American distributors. He had gone to his great reward by the time I showed up, but not before earning his store a great reputation. For his son, I came to be the American wine buyer.

In that capacity I got to know all manner of West Coast wineries. I followed their wines year after year and met their producers. The District, a federal territory, had liberal laws that let MacArthur's buy straight from smaller wineries who had no national distribution, and I took full advantage of this. I visited the wineries, made purchases, organized the annual California Barrel Tasting the store held in Washington to sell wine futures, stocked shelves, and sold wine to customers. But increasingly I found myself drawn to France and its wine, rather than the wine I was directly responsible for. And increasingly I found myself intensely frustrated with the dust.

By this time, my parents were retiring to a farm they had bought in Virginia's Shenandoah Valley. In July of 1997 they flew to France to take a biking holiday with friends. Three days later, riding too fast down a steep road in Burgundy's countryside, my father fell headlong over the handlebars and landed in an intensive care ward in a Dijon hospital. He lay deep in a coma when I flew out days later. This was my first visit to France since hitch-hiking there as a student during a year abroad in London. I got a car in Paris, drove to Dijon without mishap, and found Mom at her hotel. For a week I joined her vigil while waiting for the ambulance plane to come take Dad to a hospital in Charlottesville.

In August, back in Washington and with no change in Dad's condition, I met with the sales director of a California winery. I had done business with him for several years, and we enjoyed a good relationship. He had penciled out a scheme to start an import company, and he needed a buyer. The District was something of a hotbed of importers, and he figured that I was well connected, so months earlier he had asked me to set up interviews with potential candidates. This I did, and accompanied him to make the introductions. The meetings went nowhere, however—nobody wanted to take a chance on a new importing company—and so in the end I threw the dice. I asked him why he didn't just offer me the job.

He thought that was a pretty good idea.

It wasn't, not really. I was deemed to have a good palate and had plenty of experience as a buyer. But I was, as I said, the American wine buyer, and while my passion for wine had certainly gravitated toward European wine, and French wine above all, over the years, I had no contacts in France. I had never done business there. I had no experience importing wine. And then there was the language problem.

But I didn't dwell on these things. I had just come back from France and lived to tell the tale. That became my rock. Anything was possible—*it had to be.* No one knew if Dad would survive, and if he did emerge from his coma, there was, among the doctors, no confidence whatsoever that he would ever be the same. That was the deal; that was what I was facing. In light of that, taking a leap of faith on a new job, however laden it might be with responsibility, didn't seem so difficult.

Such bravado bespoke how raw I felt at the time. But taking that leap did create its own momentum, and it pulled me out of my professional rut, to borrow from W. H. Murray. Murray's words were framed on a wall at home, and they resonated keenly with me during those days. Of all things, he was a Scottish mountain climber. In 1951 he wrote in his book, *The Scottish Himalayan Expedition*:

> . . . but when I said that nothing had been done I erred in one important matter. We had definitely committed ourselves and were halfway out of our ruts. We had put down our passage money—booked a sailing to Bombay. This may sound too simple, but is great in consequence. Until one is committed, there is hesitancy, the chance to draw back, always ineffectiveness. Concerning all acts of initiative (and creation), there is one elementary truth, the ignorance of which kills

countless ideas and splendid plans: that the moment one definitely commits oneself, then providence moves too. A whole stream of events issues from the decision, raising in one's favor all manner of unforeseen incidents and meetings and material assistance, which no man could have dreamt would have come his way. I have learned a deep respect for one of Goethe's couplets:

Whatever you can do or dream you can, begin it. Boldness has genius, power, and magic in it.

My new company's management ignored my deficits as willingly as I did. Thus I went off to France with shreds of high school French under my belt and a few faxed appointments in hand. What saved me was Joe — providence, it seems, tapped *him* on the shoulder. Long ago Joe had spent a year at France's University of Besançon to learn the language. He saw immediately that, deaf and dumb, I stood to perish in the wilderness, and he announced his wish to come and lend a verbal hand. Ostensibly, he saw this as too good an adventure to pass up (it was). But behind the adventure, I imagine that he also wanted to pay homage to Dad, and going to France to help his kid brother would do that and at the same time give a measure of hope to Mom. Moreover, I think he had to do something, anything. The same forces that compelled me worked their discord on him. My job had lost its meaning during the same time that his marriage had crumbled, and now our father's life lay in limbo.

I let the sales director of the winery in on the secret of Joe's presence, and he elected to keep this matter to himself. Joe was a phantom passenger who shared my car and hotel room, and who (justly) never showed up on my expense account or (unjustly) in my reports.

Chapter 2

SANCERRE

A brisk autumn morning found us driving down a *route nationale* amid pockets of fog on our first full day in France. Back then the A-77 autoroute to the upper Loire Valley was being built, so south of Paris we had to take a more intimate secondary road. This was a fine thing so far as we were concerned, for we were all eyes at this new world. (Later I would learn that this road, the N-7, had been *the* route for Parisians to the Côte d'Azur during the summer holidays until the advent of the modern autoroutes, and had as much a place in history for the French as Route 66 had for Americans.) The road gave us time to take in the feel of the landscape, one that gained gentle folds and rolls as we came into the upper Loire Valley. The vast agricultural fields and orderly woodlands that lay south of Paris gave way to hedge-rowed pastures and compact stone villages. To a green American with imagination, these villages appeared out of the fog with a surreal quality, framing a rural way of life that had seemingly changed little since the days of Joan of Arc. The air was chilled. Wood smoke mingled with the moist smell of fallen leaves and wet earth. This was land that was at once enchanting, forbidding, and fecund.

"*Je sens la France!*" Joe announced upon filling his lungs with a mighty draft. He sat in the passenger seat, his arms raised in a halfhearted burst of energy. He let them fall into his lap. He rubbed his eyes. "*Sentir,*" he explained, "to smell. It also means to be conscious of something. It's related to our words 'sense' and 'sentimentality.' It's a great verb." He yawned hugely. "French," he added as an afterthought, "is all about nuance."

Joe's head was full of such detail. He was the repository of knowledge in the family. He crossed his hands over his stomach, leaned his head back, and closed his eyes. He inhaled again deeply. "*Je sens un champ de merde,*" he said.

"What?" I asked.

"I smell a field of shit," he said. He pointed to a pasture of cows on his side of the road. He guffawed blearily, sitting back up. "Coffee, Roy," he said. "We need coffee."

We had arrived the morning before. Joe had flown from Seattle, I had flown from the District, and neither of us had slept on the planes. We didn't sleep much overnight in Paris either. This journey to meet growers would prove to be about many things, but rarely would it be about rest.

No matter. We were doing the journey together. In spite of all my trepidation about going to France, my brother made this journey an adventure, and that changed everything. Had I been alone, this time could have been all too grim, something I understood innately without having put words to it. By myself, I may well have not even bothered to stop and honor the first milestone. But with Joe, I parked the car, and we walked out onto a little country bridge to lean against its railing. With a certain gravitas, we looked upon the great Loire River. I had crossed the river on that hitchhiking trip from England to Spain during my college year abroad, but my memory of it had long since fallen by the wayside.

The Loire is France's longest river, beginning deep in the Massif Central where it flows north out of the mountains and then, at Orléans, turns a corner for the Atlantic. It runs for 630 miles. It is commonly considered to mark the ancient frontier between southerners who spoke the *langue d'oc* and northerners who spoke the *langue d'oïl*. (Both translate as *tongue/language of yes*: the former is Occitan, the latter Gallo-Roman, and the Gallo-Roman dialect won the day to become modern French. As for the Loire being the border, it turns out that the more accurate line lay farther south, but that's of no consequence here.) It was a central highway for the Gauls, the Romans, the Visigoths, and the Franks. Its valley was the stage on which century upon century of French history played out and gave birth to the nation. That valley is France's heartland.

It was also, on this overcast, jet-lagged morning, just a lazy, languid river flowing down a broad, languid valley. We stood on that bridge quietly, the car parked back on land to the side of the road. After a moment, Joe asked, "How do you say 'bottle' again?"

Inwardly, I sighed. "Bo-tay," I said.

"*Boo*-tay!" he corrected.

"Boo-tay," I repeated. "Boo-tay. *La* boo-tay."

"Right. Feminine. Good job."

He looked at the river. I looked at the river. As brothers, we were barely more than a year and a half apart, because in her early days our mother had been a practicing Catholic until our father, after a handful of kids in rapid succession, thought it the better part of valor to get himself a vasectomy and have the family join a Unitarian congregation (his life was writ large with such bold strokes). We were the middle two siblings; a sister stood on either side of us. Physically, Joe was bigger than I was. He had our grandfather's stocky build where I had our father's slight frame. He had a beard and a thick head of brown hair where I was clean-shaven and had fine sandy hair.

"You know," I said, "I expected something grander."

"Yeah?" Joe asked. "I don't know. Look at this river—look at those floodplains. Look at the width. Did you know that this is the only big river in France that's never been dammed? This thing must be a mother after a big snowpack melt or after some serious rain."

When it came to nature, Joe was passionate. He observed it closely and took many a cue from it. Nature grounded him.

"The only thing they've done to this waterway," he added, "was to build these big-assed dikes along its banks farther down in the central part of the valley to contain the water. For a country this old, they could have done a lot worse in the way of heavy-handed engineering."

"Okay," I said. "Fair enough. Did you know there's something like sixty different wine appellations along this river?"

He considered that. He rubbed his beard. "Sixty?" he asked.

"Sixty-seven," I said.

"That's a lot of wine," he allowed.

I looked down at the little silt islands in the water and the vast sandbars. The river had high banks with scrubby flatlands below and floodplains above. It probably *was* a mother in a flood. "All right," I said, stepping back from the railing. "Let's get to Sancerre and have that coffee before we have to start tasting."

"Coffee?" Joe said. "Heck, maybe we ought to be men about it and go right to the wine. Sixty-seven appellations? We've got a lot of work ahead of us!"

We laughed, heading for the Renault. We both remembered Renaults back in the '70s and when they were imported to the States. They were terrible cars in those days (then again, most cars were). But this new Renault rental was a fine vehicle. It took us confidently across the Loire and toward the hills. The fog lifted; the day brightened. We drove through the riverside village of St. Satur, over which stood a startlingly high railroad bridge. The bridge probably dated from the turn of the nineteenth century, but it was built in the manner of Roman aqueducts, with grand stone arches and stone pillars, and it straddled the chasm in which the little village sat with aplomb. We passed underneath and came to the end of the village and a roundabout. On the far side sprawled a crappy modern supermarket with an adjacent fast-food joint and a gas station, all bordering a beat-up parking lot. It was decidedly not something out of Joan of Arc's era. A great hill rose steeply on our left, and Joe craned his neck to see to the top. "Hot dog," he said. "Sancerre!"

The town crowned the hill. I put the car in gear, and we climbed the long flank and then drove alongside the ancient ramparts forming the crown. We went by the modern Hôtel Panoramic and around to the front of the commanding hill. As untold numbers had before us, we stopped there for the view. Below, St. Satur's nimble railroad bridge stepped high above the village and curved over the chasm like the centerpiece of an enthusiast's painstakingly built model train system. In the distance, the fat Loire—now a pleasingly pastoral sight—meandered through verdant lowlands. On the river's far side lay the appellation of Pouilly-Fumé, Sancerre's rival in wine but no match, it was plain to see, in landscape. It was on our side that the land flexed its muscles; Pouilly-Fumé had none of the sinewy hills and dales of the Sancerre appellation.

Behind us, in the shade of stately flat-topped cedars, rose Sancerre's main gate. It was inscribed as *Porte César*. I wondered about Caesar. I knew that he marched up the Rhône Valley to modern-day Burgundy and established Beaune as a military encampment. From there, the Romans moved northwest to England and northeast to Alsace and into Germany, but what direction Caesar himself took I had no clue. Beaune, however, was east-southeast of Sancerre, about a two-and-a-half-hour drive in the late twentieth century. It was entirely possible that Caesar had come here.

"You think Caesar was here?" I asked the repository of knowledge.

"I have no idea," Joe answered. "But this hill must have had one kind of fort after another since who-knows-when. If he came this way, he probably stopped here."

That made sense. He who controlled the hill controlled the river and its transport. Before the Romans, there were the Gauls, and they almost certainly had an outpost on Sancerre's high ground. In more modern days, Sancerre was a Protestant stronghold and was sacked twice during the Wars of Religion. The first time was in 1573 after a seven-month siege; the second time was in 1621. The second attack saw the destruction of the castle, save for its twelfth-century tower. After that, the Protestant Huguenots pretty much split town.

Those weren't the best of times to live. Life had to have been better during the Roman occupation (unless you were a slave), when the ever-practical Romans recognized Sancerre's well-drained, south-facing hillsides as fine vineyard land and planted vines. "Well," I said, feeling astute, "a hilltop fort, a river highway, and lots of local wine. What more did a Roman need?"

"Cheese," answered Joe. "We're in the land of *croûton de Chavignol*." He spoke these words with a perfect

French accent: *Krouw-tohn de Cha-vee-nohl.* It was maddening how he could do that. In the weeks before boarding the plane, I had tried to brush up on my French but quickly despaired. To learn to speak with Joe's skill required discipline, time, aptitude, and fortitude to counter an onslaught of inadequacy. It required dedication to slog through the linguistic French minefield. Not least, it required an ability to enunciate clearly. I tend to mumble. Joe, however, took zero notice of such perils. He slapped my arm. "The French," he explained, apparently fired up by the mention of cheese, "have an earthy sense of humor. You see, a crouton is a dropping, as in the pieces of toast you drop on a salad. Around here, they make neat little molds of goat cheese and call them croutons from the village of Chavignol. Meanwhile, the goats themselves leave neat little droppings of turd all over the place."

I looked at him. "It's that nuance thing," he said. He shrugged. "Let's get that coffee and look around."

He liked to explore. We both did. We passed through the port to Sancerre's main square where we stopped at a bar for shots of strong, bitter coffee. The square was rectangular in shape and sloping, and sometime in very recent history a modern tourist office had been dug into the middle of the slope to look cavelike upon the lower end of the square, with new cobblestone laid on its level roof for outdoor cafe seating. It was an ugly practical improvement. We got back into the car and drove through the narrow and far better preserved streets. At the highest point in Sancerre rises the castle tower, in a park surrounded by more of those looming flat-topped cedars. That morning the park was closed. Nonetheless, we climbed out of the car to look upon the old structure towering above its green garden, its stone almost black in the wintry light. It looked altogether cold and uninviting.

The surrounding hamlets beckoned: Sury-en-Vaux, Maimbray, Verdigny, Chavignol, and Bué—wine villages all, none more so than Bué. We drove out of town and along the saddle of Sancerre's hill, then down the back side to turn into a pocket canyon and so into Bué. There was no mistaking the livelihood of the village; over just about every door hung a shingle declaring the name of a wine grower's domaine, or farm.

There we found Domaine Vincent Pinard, our first appointment. Suddenly, I was intensely nervous. So was Joe. We had never called on a French domaine before. Our jet-lagged bodies were wracked, and we struggled to exude a calm professionalism. I longed for a drink of water. We knocked on the door. The lady of the house appeared, a questioning look in her eyes. Joe immediately stuttered, his tongue flaying his palate without coherent result. His face flushed red. Our professionalism was shattered. At last, Joe got out who we were, whereupon *Madame* issued a torrent of French and pointed around the corner. Vincent was in back in the winery. As we walked around, I asked, "Was that the nuance thing you were doing just then?"

"My mind," he said, shaking his head, "it just froze!"

In back, Vincent Pinard was concluding business with a private client, who happily stuffed cases of wine into the trunk of his car. The client drove off with a wave, and Vincent turned to us with a warm smile. He was a trim, bearded man, and he led us into his small winery, convivially talking to Joe, whose brain had thankfully started to thaw.

I found myself warming as well, for tasting in wineries (American ones, anyway) was something I knew. Inside Pinard's winery, square, squat, steel vats lined one wall, and my memory has them painted red, while the concrete floor was painted white. Everything had just been sprayed down, and a sheen of water coated the floor. By the end of the day Joe and I would remark that the Sancerrois are a tidy people, and their cellars are typically immaculate. Spraying down a cellar before a client's visit was standard practice, like the sweeping of the doorstep before company arrived.

Vincent opened a tiny spigot to a vat and filled three glasses with a mouthful of that year's Sauvignon Blanc, the white wine of Sancerre. It was a shock so early in the morning: piercingly fresh, with crisp pungent grapefruit flavors that cascaded over our palates like a bracing mountain stream over stones. That sounds hokey, I know, but it's true—there was this revitalizing sense of minerality about the wine.

Years later, I tasted Pinard's neighbor Thierry Merlin's Sancerre *classique* with an experienced retailer, who remarked favorably that the wine had "that whole lemon-oyster shell thing going on." He understood that Sancerre's soils have an extraordinarily thick layer of decomposed

oyster shells from a time long before the Roman occupation, when the area was a seabed. Sancerre resides within
the Paris Basin, which once contained a giant sea whose
boundary can be traced from Sancerre northeast to
Chablis and Champagne, and west to southern England.
At hillside road cuts in Sancerre or Champagne, you can
see the white, chalky soil—the same seashell-infused
limestone soil that makes up the white cliffs of Dover in
England.

Politely, Vincent looked at us to gauge our reaction.
He needn't have. Joe all but whistled, while I was captivated even before I spit the wine into a floor drain. Today,
the upper Loire Valley vies with Bordeaux for the honor
of producing France's best Sauvignon Blanc, but the
lamentable fact is that the wine of either region makes a
mockery of the Sauvignon Blanc produced in California.
Californian Sauvignon, by and large, stinks. It invariably
lacks freshness and *vif*, or liveliness. In large part this is
because most of the variety is planted in rich sites that are
too hot. But the problem is also cultural, because freshness in wine is grounded in acidity, and acid is the big
bugaboo of the typical American wine drinker. *It's sour*,
the sourpuss says, and goes back to his white Zinfandel
or soda pop.

And by and large, American winemakers and their
marketers have slavishly followed sourpuss into medioc-
rity, at least when it comes to Sauvignon Blanc. The only
American Sauvignon that truly caught my attention was
made by Philip Togni, an independently minded small

grower if ever there was one. From a tiny vineyard on top of Napa Valley's often downright cold Spring Mountain, he made a wine that held its own against fine Sancerre, full of cut (to use a nice English term about acid) and zesty-rich body. His wine had what every other rendition made down on the valley floor did not: an innate concentration of fresh fruit. Appropriately enough, he sold most of it to the Oyster Bar in Manhattan's Grand Central Station. Philip understood that a good balance of acid—given naturally by the vineyard site rather than added from a bag—is a prerequisite in white wine, if the wine is to have elevated perfume, if it is to refresh and cleanse the palate between bites of food, and if it is to hold the interest of he who imbibes.

Unfortunately, his vineyard succumbed to a disease and is no more. But he showed what was possible.

Vincent Pinard tasted us through all the vats of what would become his base, or classic, wine. We then moved to what he considered to be the finer lots, made partly or entirely in small oak barrels rather than in steel vats. This is where we parted company. I would have far preferred to see him using old *foudre*—oversize casks that allow the wine to breathe and gain in complexity without imparting ponderous wood flavors and bitter oak tannins. Putting a crisp white wine such as Sancerre into young oak barrels has always been self-defeating to me, but one man's poison can be another man's passion.

We left with samples in hand and drove through the village. On three sides, vineyards climbed the hills, and at the head of the hollow stood Bué's sober little church and the somber memorial to its men felled in the First World War. But such things did not touch us. "Damn, Joe," I said. "I just might be able to do this!" Joe, who had rediscovered his treasured French, smiled broadly, pushed back his thick hair, and punched the air in victory. It didn't hurt that we had a little buzz going from the wine, despite not swallowing. We zoomed out of the village and up into the vineyards, the world our oyster.

The bite proved to be short-lived, however. We spent the rest of the day tasting in Verdigny, and as the day waned, so did my enthusiasm. None of the domaines we visited won me over. They all made good, commercial wines, but none inspired. Indeed, it became clear that the Sancerrois knew all too well that they had a viable commodity in their wine, and most seemed to take the approach that all they had to do was not screw it up. There was an abundance of new cellars, gleaming stainless steel tanks, and well-heeled proprietors who made straightforward, confident wine that never quite had any *there* there, as Gertrude Stein would say. Their wines were all but indistinguishable from one another. Tasting them became depressing, and I began to think that I was getting nowhere.

We ended the day at Domaine Thomas & Fils, our appointments in Sancerre finished. Weeks earlier, the domaine's American importer, Bobby Kacher, had invited me to meet him, for it turned out that we were going to be in Sancerre at the same time. He lived in Washington and I had known him since the late 1980s. We found him there with a handful of his customers in tow. They regarded us with thinly disguised competition, but it was heartening to see Bobby's familiar face in this foreign land. He introduced us to Jean Thomas (the *fils*) and his wife, Ginette. Ginette disappeared inside, and Jean led the customers down into his cellar. Bobby, for his part, unzipped his pants, turned his back, and pissed mightily into the Thomases' bushes. Joe's eyes popped. He looked at me and nodded with apparent approval toward the spectacle, as if to point out that France had options, tangible options, other than just nuance to recommend it. Then Bobby finished his business and ushered us underground for yet another tasting.

Jean had just built himself a new cellar, and we stayed some time in that vast, chilly concrete bunker. Upon ascending, we found that night had fallen. A numbing cold lay over the land and took our breath away. Verdigny backs up against a steep hillside to look south over two long, fat swells of hills rolling one after the other toward Sancerre, which sits aloof on its pedestal. That lodestar, however, was now a mere twinkle of lights in the ice-cold darkness. Inside the Thomas household, Ginette discreetly took Joe and me aside in the hall to tell us that she had a friend in Bué who was looking for an American importer. Did we want to see him tomorrow? We agreed to a visit first thing in the morning. Ginette slipped Joe a piece of paper with the name of the grower and disappeared to telephone her friend.

We looked at one another as if divine intervention had just shown its hand. "Holy *merde*!" Joe whispered. "You lose that," I said, "and you're sleeping in the car!"

Jean invited us into the dining room to sit with Bobby and his customers. This was my first introduction to a French farmer's hospitality. I would come to learn that business with a *vigneron* can be done from a distance, as it were, but it is once you are invited into his household for dinner that the hand is extended, and that hand can be quite loyal. It was Bobby who they had at their table, but as his guests all courtesies were extended to us.

The thing was, it was completely natural. Even the other Americans let down their guard. We all sat at the table — five or six of us — while Ginette brought out the first course and Jean opened a few bottles of wine. The pop of corks, however, tempered our excitement, and a look of resignation came over Joe's face. We were burned out on wine. It occurred to me that I was pretty much burned out period at this day's end. The rude cold outside had been a shock, and when I recovered, I found myself weakened a notch. I didn't have a whole lot of notches left.

But then the food came.

First was a dish of scallops and mussels cooked in a cream sauce infused with Pernod. Joe perked up. Finely attuned to the pleasures of a good meal, he immersed his face in the steam coming off his plate and beamed upon inhaling a great, fragrant whiff. The signal was given to proceed. In an unremitting attack, Joe and I devoured what lay on our plates. With no foes left to slay, our eyes met across the table. We both nearly burst out laughing. We glanced furtively at those eating normally around us, and then eyed the bread that lay in the basket between us. Bread is one of the great constants in French life. Bread, at that moment, looked to be the best thing to have come down the pike since canned beer. Joe's hand reached out and snagged a particularly large chunk of baguette fresh from the *boulangerie*. He ripped it in two, mopped up what appeared to be an entire reservoir of sauce with the one half, and shoved the dripping moist mouthful of bread into his maw. Then he leaned back, the better to savor his chew.

I followed suit, letting a melange of flavors roll over my tongue: succulent scallops and briny mussels, both lifted by the licorice-flavored Pernod and overlaid with the rich, mouth-coating cream sauce. I took a swallow of Sancerre and instantly the vibrant wine cut through the cream and left me licking my lips. It was a fine moment in gastronomy.

The first course was cleared and red Sancerre was poured. Red Sancerre is a popular bistro wine in Paris, but little seen in America. At the time, I had almost no experience with it. The grape is Pinot Noir, although the version here is a whole lot lighter than its American sibling, which may have something to do with its popularity in Paris. A light red wine that can be drunk at a meal without tanking its drinkers has real virtue.

Pinot Noir has been cultivated in the upper Loire for a long time. No one really knows if it goes back as far as the fifth century, when the written record has viticulture firmly established in the Loire Valley, but it well could have. Somewhere along the line, perhaps during the Duchy of Burgundy's heyday in the centuries leading up to the Wars of Religion, Pinot Noir became an important red variety in Sancerre's vineyards. At that time the upper Loire was the western edge of the duchy. Along the flank of Burgundy's famous hillside, the Côte d'Or, Pinot Noir had already been literally decreed—in 1395!—to be the one legally permitted red grape by Philippe the Bold. It is said with conviction that red was the dominant color of Sancerre's wine prior to the latter half of the 1800s, when the vine louse phylloxera jumped ship from America and devastated the Old World's vineyards. Whether that red was made solely from Pinot Noir, or was a mixture of various red grapes, is not stated with conviction. After phylloxera, however, Sauvignon Blanc took root and came to be the face of Sancerre. Today, most growers make a little Pinot Noir of varying but increasingly better quality, and a little Pinot Noir rosé, which can be neat stuff, and a whole lot of Sauvignon Blanc.

Ginette appeared next with some sort of meatball and rice course. That was followed by a cheese course, by which time Joe and I could eat no more. With the close of evening, reality descended. Tomorrow we were leaving the region, and I was running out of time. My sense of mission awoke with a vengeance. If I wasn't going to return home with a Sancerre producer signed up, then at the very least I had to get a handle on the region to make the trip worthwhile. I had to learn. So I asked the Americans at the table about the stylistic differences inherent in the Sauvignons from the surrounding hamlets. There had to be differences, I thought (there are: wines from Maimbray, for example, with its heavier clay soils, are relatively powerful and backward in youth and pointed with acidity, while those from Bué, a commune with much less clay mixed in its white, chalky limestone, are marked by elegance and perfume). Then I had a really bright idea. I offered to get the samples that we had collected during the day from the car to see if differences could be pinpointed. The response around the table was lukewarm. Being reasonable, they wanted to go to bed. I didn't get this. In fact, I was oblivious. I wanted to get my hands around the essence of Sancerre, and I walked blindly out of that safe haven.

Outside, my breath was all white frost in the black air. It was mildly alarming, how cold the night had become. I hurried to the car, fumbled with the key, and grabbed all the sample bottles from the trunk to line them up on the road. I was shocked to see that there were close to a dozen, and even I understood that that was too many. At that point, I realized that it was eleven o'clock and here I was about to open all these bottles. On the face of it, this was crazy. But I was new on the job, and responsibility weighed heavily. Besides, my thinking went, I had Kacher the importer and Thomas the grower on hand—when would I have such an audience again? This was my day in Sancerre; this was my shot! I put half the wine back in the trunk and slammed the lid shut. With three bottles per hand, I marched back to the house.

Inside, I opened every one, and the whys and hows of the merits of each went out the window as every wine was dismissed by the tired group, who spit them out with negative remarks into an ice bucket that Jean Thomas thoughtfully provided. They were right to do so; I hadn't been impressed myself. But it was impossible for me to not want to like something about these wines, because they were what I had to show for my work.

Finally, I pulled out Pinard's *classique*, which I knew to be a good wine. But by then, closing in on midnight, rebellion had clearly taken hold, and Pinard's wine was rejected as "hollow." Even Jean, obviously a kind man, shook his head.

In the morning, at the Hôtel Panoramic, I had a crisis of confidence. It was bad enough to cause waves of anxiety to ripple through me, ratcheting up my pulse while at the same time putting this enormous weight upon me. I paced up and down that little room and generally began to bug out. "I don't know, Joe," I said. "I just don't know. I really don't know."

"What don't you know?" Joe asked. He eyed me warily and sat on the bed, trying to assume a reasonable disposition.

That might have worked, except a big brother note of irritation laced his tone, which goaded me to no end.

"I just don't know," I said, continuing to pace.

"What don't you know?" he repeated.

"I don't know what I don't know, goddamnit. What don't you know?"

"Me? I don't know what's going on!"

"That makes two of us," I said, too angry to be anxious any longer. "Let's get out of this *tiny room*."

We grabbed our bags, paid the bill in sour silence, and climbed into the car with headaches and bad moods. It was freezing cold too. Fog was everywhere, a damp, chilly presence that hung over the land as if produced by dry ice on the second-rate movie set of a medieval landscape. I drove out of Sancerre and down the back of the ridge toward Bué, thinking that this weather was worse than any northern European winter day I remembered from my year in England. That seemed like a terrifically long time ago, which didn't help my mood much because if it really was that long ago, then I was that much closer to the grave.

But England made me think of King Arthur. I thought of *Monty Python and the Holy Grail*. I thought of the king in the movie traveling with his servant who knocked coconuts together to imitate the sound of horse hooves clacking on cobblestone, and how they clacked their way to the castle defended by a Frenchman who swore at the English with a thick French accent. Maybe, it occurred to me, that was it: If I spoke with a French accent, maybe I could master this Mount Everest of a language. That was a thought.

"*Boo-tay,*" I muttered, trying it out.

"What?" Joe asked sharply.

"*Boo-tay ∂e vaigh,*" I said. "*Boooo-tay ∂e vaigh!*" I exclaimed, lifting my hands high above the steering wheel.

Joe stared implacably at me.

"I am speeking zee Franche," I said, reclaiming the wheel. "Dis iz how eet iz done, no?"

A silence befell us. What I was doing was so absurd that I didn't know whether to laugh or cry. Joe began coughing. His face turned purple, as if he were having a heart attack. But he wasn't. He was laughing.

"Ah," I continued, inspired, "I see zee krab, he has grabbed your ass. *Mon ∂ieu,* eet must hurt!"

"You!" he spit out. "You sound like a castrated Swiss banker!" He coughed a final time. He collapsed back into his seat, breathing deeply. He regained his composure. "I can't believe I signed on for this," he said.

"Come on," I said, "there's hope! I could do worse. I could sound like a castrated Chinese banker!"

Giddily, we turned into Bué. Into the winding hollow we drove and found Ginette's tip, Domaine Merlin-Cherrier, right there across the street from Pinard's place. In fact, Pinard could have easily walked out of his house and seen these disheveled, grinning foreign brothers who had come only yesterday now parking in front of his rival neighbor's house. That could have been disconcerting, so we straightened up.

Thierry Merlin's house is built directly on one of the hollow's flanks. His cellar burrows into it, his house perches above it, and a parcel of his vines runs straight down that steep hillside to his rear door. He met us that frigid, foggy morning coming out of his garage, wiping tractor grease from his hand, a tall, handsome man with an easy and honest demeanor. He apologized for the grease and invited us into his cellar through the big door at street level. Instinctively, I liked the fact that this man had grease on his hand.

Inside were two small chambers packed with a handful of steel tanks of various sizes. A third chamber was under construction, its entrance draped in plastic sheeting. Thierry waved his hand toward the plastic that hid what would become his bottling and storage chamber, apologizing for the dirt and dust.

Glasses were passed around and the first tank tapped. This, Thierry said, was the wine from a parcel he farmed over in communal Sancerre, where the soil was heavier and sprinkled with flint. Citrus notes exploded from the glass, and the Sauvignon fruit was fat, succulent, and immediately appealing. Then the wine fell short, the flavor disappearing in the blink of an eye.

The next tank held the harvest from a limestone vineyard named *Les Garannes* in Bué. This was leaner, with terrific finesse and length; a lovely wine that was clearly the finer of the two.

The third tank contained wine made from a parcel of old vines Thierry had growing on top of the hill behind the house. Here he described chalky limestone soil strewn with what the locals called *griottes*, literally "cherries" but referring to pebbles. He noted that the vines dated from the 1950s. This wine was dense, rich, and long with old-vine intensity. I said as much to Joe, who said as much to Thierry, who smiled. He added that these two tanks, the second and third, were his kind of wine; he wasn't enamored by the wine in the first tank. But taken as a whole, as we would see, the different wines would make a fine *classique*.

The fourth tank held the wine from the famed Chêne Marchand vineyard. This gravelly chalk vineyard occupies the plateau immediately to the west of the village. They say the site may have been a vineyard since Roman times. The plateau overlooks a plain to the south and is protected by higher hills to the north, and the vines bask in sun all the day long — if the day offers sun to ripen fruit, which can't be taken for granted. All of the Loire's important wine appellations are firmly in northern Europe, a far cry from France's sunny Midi on the Mediterranean coast. As a result, incisive elegance is the supreme virtue of good Loire wine, while watery acidity is the vice of lousy Loire wine. What you get in a bottle depends on the year, the grower, and the site. Down through the centuries, Chêne Marchand has proven itself the surest site in Bué for succulently ripening grapes.

Thierry had acquired two parcels, totaling just two acres of vines. He's a small grower, working thirty-five acres, so what he has in Chêne is not insignificant. More importantly for a *vigneron* in Bué, Chêne represents a great legacy, a patrimony passed down through the ages, although this isn't always respected. The larger of the two parcels Thierry inherited from his grandfather, the smaller one he purchased, and both were in bad shape. The vines were diseased and the soil exhausted by synthetic fertilizers. Equally bad, the parcels had not been tilled in years. The previous generation had been content to ride tractors through the rows, hauling a sprayer and fertilizer distributor, compacting the soil into something resembling cement. Such was the fashion of the time.

So Thierry ripped out the impoverished vines and tilled. He planted deep-rooted grasses to aerate the soil and other cover crops to replenish nutrients. He did this again and again for an astonishing ten years (I learned this fact from this modest man long after I began working with him). Finally, he judged the soil ready for vines.

For the first few years he vinified the juice separately but blended it into his *classique* Sancerre rather than bottling it as a vineyard designated wine. Then he began to do something special. He put all the juice from his two little parcels into one small tank and let the fermentation take its course naturally with the indigenous yeast that came in on the grapes. He left the wine on its fine lees for twelve to fourteen months, depending on whether the summer had yielded meager or generous grapes. The result is a particularly elegant Sancerre with a nose of lemon blossom, then spice and hazelnuts, and (with some age) a touch of honey, and layered flavors that unfold subtly, underpinned by minerality. The hallmark of all of France's great white wines is richness coupled with minerality, and Thierry's Chêne has a wonderful vein of stone. The wine has an understated sense of finesse and power that comes from Bué's chalk-infused limestone soils. In that way, his Chêne epitomizes the best of Bué's wines.

He took us up to the Chêne Marchand plateau in his four-wheeler. When I say plateau, the image in this case should be the gently rolling top of a long mound of a hill forming one side of the horseshoe that snugly cloisters Bué on three sides. We lingered up there longer than we should have, given the day's pressing schedule. But the fog was slowly burning off, and Joe and I knew we had found something in Thierry. So we stood and talked before the few rows of vines that, for this man, represented the apogee of everything that he had ever worked for.

Then he asked us where we were headed. "Burgundy," Joe replied.

"Ah, the Burgundians," said Thierry knowingly. A smile creased his face mischievously. "Don't they still walk on their paws?"

Chapter 3

AVALLON

*I*n Europe, analogies are often made between a region's people and its food. If the Sancerrois are like their neat balls of austere goat cheese, then Burgundians resemble their *époisse:* little wheels of strong, smelly cow's milk cheese frequently so runny that they must be contained in a box. One is likeable and readily comprehended; the other is more layered and needs time to be understood.

As we left Sancerre that cold, wintry morning, neither Joe nor I had yet made this connection. All we knew was that we were headed toward the mecca of French viticulture (the Bordelais would take issue with that, but commercially Bordeaux long ago became the Wall Street of French viticulture). There has long been a sense of grandeur about Burgundy, a region that bequeathed its vineyards such illustrious names as Chambertin, Corton-Charlemagne, and Montrachet. These were but three of Burgundy's thirty grand crus. Each had seized my imagination years before, and in my mind's eye I could place where they lay in relation to the twenty-odd villages with equally impressive names (Chambolle-Musigny, Vosne-Romanée, and Volnay, to name a few) that lined the narrow, thirty-mile-long flank of hillside known as the Côte d'Or. I was familiar with the wines of these villages, and I knew their individual reputations. But I had never been to the Côte.

The sense of grandeur surrounding Burgundy is real. It's an ancient region of dukes and nobility, of pomp and pageantry, and its traditions have been passed down through the centuries with remarkable coherence. In the small town of Beaune you can find every strata of Burgundian society, from stalwart peasants to regal nobility, who bicker and gossip endlessly but who are united by a deeply ingrained regional identity. They are a proud people.

But, as I say, I didn't know any of this yet. All I knew firsthand about Burgundy was that its capital city of Dijon had a hospital with a brain trauma wing that was, at first glance, dishearteningly primitive. The television image I carried of sleek, modern hospitals staffed with self-assured doctors didn't pan out. Dijon's trauma wing was housed just outside the old city in a single-story annex built on the cheap sometime during the first half of the twentieth century. We would walk there every day, Mom and I, from Le Chapeau Rouge, a small, upscale hotel, to the dismal annex where Dad lay hooked up to a breathing machine alongside other coma patients. Many of the patients looked all too young, their paths cut short by a car or motorcycle accident. Like my father, they writhed unconsciously in discontent. Nothing about the place felt right.

Dijon proper is also idiosyncratic. It's a small city laced by narrow one-way streets. It has a thriving market and inviting cafes (in one I saw my first rosy-cheeked old man in a beret fortifying himself with a kir at ten in the morning while we had our coffee—a sight I would have thought staged had I seen it in a movie). It also has La Place de François Rude. There was the much more grandiose Dukes' Palace and parade square, but it was François Rude's cobblestone square that I kept returning to. Here, surrounding the whimsical statue of a boy treading grapes, were outdoor cafes and a nearby church with a big bell and a mechanical man who popped out upon the hour to bong the bell. MFK Fisher described Dijon as a damp, dark, ugly provincial town, but she held obvious affection for the place. In her book *Long Ago in France,* she wrote with an eager and trenchant eye of her formative years between the wars in that ancient city. It's an evocative book, and I read it with numb curiosity during those days of waiting for the ambulance plane to come for Dad.

Mom and I would meet for breakfast, and afterward she would check in with American Express to see how the arrangements were going with the plane. Then we would walk down to the hospital annex to see if this would be a new day, if there had been any change overnight. Each time, we met with the one brain trauma doctor who spoke English (there was another on staff, but he had no more

English than we had French). Each time, he counseled patience. Every day we had lunch at a different cafe, and every night we had dinner at another restaurant to enjoy what we could of Burgundy. But of course it seemed wrong to be looking for enjoyment. I found it difficult to get my arms around the fact that my father was horribly injured. It became a welcome escape at the end of the day to open *Long Ago in France* and read about Dijon in an earlier era. Fisher wrote authoritatively and with a retrospective air of resignation that offered solace.

Driving across the flatlands toward Burgundy from Sancerre, Joe and I talked about that book. MFK Fisher was a wonderful writer: deft, laconic, and insightful. She is known for her writings on food, but it would be a mistake to think that she wrote simply about food. Food for her was a metaphor for life: One eats, therefore one is. She never lost sight of that truth, and she wrote about it with an especially sensual relish. In the 1950s she returned to Dijon for a food fair. After attending various extended banquets, she sneaked off to have a meal alone at Crespin, her favorite restaurant in the early 1930s. It had survived, she notes, as she had, and her sense of urgency dissipated upon walking through Crespin's doors:

> I settled myself comfortably at the table and picked up the menu with politeness, knowing exactly what I would order. This I did, and it was good: a dozen *Portugaises Vertes Extra,* then a dozen snails, then some ripe cheese from the Cistercian Abbey not far away.

I drank a glass of dry white vermouth first, nothing with the almost violently alive sea-tasting oysters, and a half-bottle of red Meursault of a good year but somewhat disappointing. . . .

The heavy-legged kind waitress tended me with the slightly worried solicitude of a nurse whose patient looks normal enough but exhibits peculiar symptoms: Did I really want a red Meursault and not a white? And did I really want a dozen of *both* the oysters and the snails, no little grilled *biftec*, no *Coq au Chambertin*? And was I sure I meant the Cistercian or had I intended to say Camembert? Yes, yes, I said . . . red, yes, no, yes, and went on eating and drinking pleasurably, warmed by the being there even more than by the nourishment.

The wine picked up a bit with the cheese, and then *I sat back*, as I had done so often and so well in Crespin. Coffee was black and brutal.

Such words made us hungry. Moreover, we had spent the better part of an early hour tasting Thierry Merlin's bracing wines, and when wine writers talk about appetizing acidity, well, that's no joke.

By the time we reached the wayward city of Clamecy, our appetites were whet and honed to a knife edge. We stopped in front of a *charcuterie*, the answer to our prayers. Inside, Joe pointed to a loaf of country pâté, and the lady indicated a portion with her knife and Joe said no, a little larger please, and she smiled and cut off a great mouthwatering slab. This she wrapped in wax paper and placed into my outstretched hands. We bought bread from a baker and found a small grocery where we loaded up with jars of cornichons and mustard, and a couple liters of water. We sped out of town, loot in hand. A few miles away, we came across a quiet pasture with a place to pull over, and there we wolfed down makeshift sandwiches in the warm car. Outside, it was cold and damp.

"Ah, Royboy!" Joe declared. "Sharp Dijon mustard, crisp little pickles, earthy, rib-sticking pâté, all sandwiched within a fine, crusty baguette . . . *mon frère*, that's good eating!" He beamed, his bearded cheeks folded back in a Cheshire cat grin. In the car, it was as if we were home again even if that time had been half our lives ago. Now, Joe was an urban planner and designer with a degree in landscape architecture from Harvard. He had a son and daughter in Seattle and had just gone through a painful divorce. I didn't know the details, and he didn't talk about them — the pain was just self-evident. The son was a savvy and rebellious snowboarder; the daughter was an athlete and an ace student. For Joe, college tuitions loomed. His profession paid poorly, however, and the mere thought of the money for colleges would drop him right into an angry, dark slough of frustration. He was susceptible to such sloughs. We stepped out of the car laughing into that dank afternoon to shed carpets of crumbs from our laps. It was our third day in France and our nerves were frayed. We were immensely excited, tired, and charged with emotion — to our eyes, the pasture before us in the overcast light was lushly green and beautiful. We stood there for a moment to take it in. All of this new land was like that: immediate, vivid, unique. We could not have perceived it any other way.

"Did you know," I said, "that the first night Mom and Dad were in Dijon they went to the coolest square in the town, sat at an outdoor cafe, and drank Beaujolais with Walt and Mary Ann? The old man, Mr. Iron Palate, drinking Beaujolais! The restaurant served it by the pitcher, and they probably drank a whole gallon of it."

"Hey," Joe said, "on vacation in France, everything tastes good."

I smiled at that. "Everything tastes good," I echoed.

Fortified by pâté sandwiches, we continued on. After Clamecy, the flatland gave way to the hills of Morvan. We came upon the village of Vézelay high on its throne, its ancient cathedral occupying the point nearest the heavens. It was in this cathedral, with the King of France in the audience, that one of the primary calls to arms for the launching of the Second Crusade was preached in 1146. A host of knights on horseback led an endless, straggling train of foot soldiers, servants, spare horses, and supply wagons lurching off that mighty outcropping of rock after receiving the blessings of Christendom. Or so we imagined it, a strange spectacle in our minds that happened here long ago, while we sped over the same hill 851 years later to wind our way toward Avallon.

How to take the full measure and meaning of time was much on our minds. As a destination, Avallon was an inchoate journey by two sons. We had no reason to go there, except that was where Dad had spilled from his bike. It was on the way to Beaune, true, but I think we would have gone there had it not been because it was our unscripted pilgrimage. Later I would come to learn that Avallon (sometimes spelled Avalon) referred to the paradise of the dead in ancient Welsh mythology, and in more general Celtic mythology this became an island paradise where King Arthur and other heroes went at death or to recover from their wounds. This would have suited our father just fine. But the reality was that he came here and got wounded instead of healed, and this Burgundian town was a long way from Wales.

We drove along in increasingly somber moods. I found myself thinking about Sancerre and Thierry Merlin. I counted myself lucky to have stumbled upon him; he was a farmer who took a considered pride in his work. As I navigated the road to Avallon, I decided that I wouldn't work with men or women I couldn't trust, and I wouldn't work with jerks, regardless of how fabulous their wine might be. The magic of wine does not exist in a vacuum; that magic is defined by the place the wine comes from and by the personality behind it. I was feeling pretty strongly about such things at that moment. I was with my brother in a foreign land with more than our share of uncertainty, and this fired me up a lot more than I understood.

We went on to find the hill where Dad rode too fast and lost control on the edge of Avallon, on a road dropping steeply down into a little gorge formed by the town's stream. On the approach to the gorge, the road was in good shape, but on the drop itself the asphalt was badly rippled and pitted. The road had not been resurfaced in years, and no one had any business flying down it. Dad was a formidable presence in our lives, a strong-willed man with, unfortunately, little experience on a bicycle. It was Joe, ironically, who knew bicycles, having raced road bikes in high school. We stepped out of the car and walked partway down the hill for lack of anything better to do. Eventually we came back up and stood around the car. After a moment, I asked, "Why the hell did he get going too fast?"

Some feet away, Joe hesitated. It was a rhetorical question. A shadow passed over his face. "He was impulsive," he said tersely. "You know that."

"He was having a good time," I said. "He got ahead of himself."

"He wasn't thinking," Joe said unwaveringly.

I didn't reply to that. I didn't want to argue. I just wanted Dad to come out of his coma. It was true that enthusiasm and purpose usually outraced fear and caution in our father. I kept up on that course with him, being cut from the same cloth, but Joe never had much of a chance. Their personalities were too different. Joe had tried, of course, being the eldest son, and he had flashes of uncontrollable anger to show for it. I never had to try; that course came naturally. Maybe too naturally, in fact, and maybe I needed to keep my guard up because this was a course that could lead to a reckless plunge that didn't end well. This thought passed over me with a chill. I glanced at Joe. His arms were crossed and he was looking down the road. I looked down there too. My eyes settled on a likely spot where the old man might have fallen. I don't know if Joe had picked out a spot as well. After a while we got back in the car and went on.

Chapter 4

BURGUNDY

e reached the A-6 and drove over the Morvan Plateau, which is grand country. Its forests change color with the seasons, but its many pastures seem forever green as any in Ireland. In the spring this verdant sea is striped by rows of vivid, yellow-headed colza, combed down the hillsides, grown to make rapeseed oil. In winter the same hillsides shoulder snow and sport bygone fortifications here and there amid forest and churches on their peaks. In the low-lying pastures stand lazy groups of creamy white Charolais cattle, the breed of Burgundy.

The autoroute crosses between the city of Auxerre and the appellation of Chablis, where Chardonnay can reach its zenith of purity. But Joe and I blew right by this northern outpost of Burgundy in our haste to get to the Côte d'Or, a name that commonly translates as the golden slope. Most take this to mean the beautiful panorama, particularly in autumn, but some could be forgiven for thinking of the gold represented by the grapes. It turns out, however, that the name is an abbreviation of Côte d'Orient, referring to the escarpment's east-facing exposition. This escarpment is the edge of the Morvan Plateau, and every morning it greets the sun rising over the vast Saône Plain.

We wanted to get there, and badly. Joe had a fine green pasture memory of wandering under the streets of Beaune in one of its subterranean wine cellars, glass in hand, wine warming his collegiate soul. Understandably, he longed to find that place again. For me, the Côte d'Or only existed in books and through flights of fancy—no shortage there, hence my desire. It had been a bitter pill that Dad's accident was the reason for my first visit to Burgundy. Now I was returning with Joe, an emboldening presence. We came not as tourists but as buyers to deal in something that had long fueled a passion in Dad and me. Three months earlier, during our vigil, Mom and I had never left Dijon. The small city's southern suburbs stop at the Côte's vines, but waiting for the ambulance plane was like waiting for Godot, a kind of purgatory that we had had no heart to break out of. The Côte was a stone's throw away, but it was a different world altogether.

Joe and I arrived toward the close of day. At Burgundy's latitude the light fades early in winter, and this had me racing down the autoroute at breakneck speed (back then, enforcement was lax and you could get away with going 100 miles per hour). We came in via Dijon, and I pointed out the dismal hospital wing. We quickly skirted it and headed down the Route Nationale 74. A couple of miles later, vineyards began taking the place of apartment buildings and commercial strips. We had entered the commune of Marsannay-la-Côte. To the left, the grasslands of the Saône Plain were at hand.

"We're here!" I exclaimed, a little stunned to realize that I could have walked here from the hospital. To the right, beyond a broad patchwork of vines, a village rose. It was silhouetted against the Côte itself, an escarpment covered in brush and scrub oak and rising abruptly. "That's got to be Marsannay," I said. Joe, atlas in hand, confirmed that it was indeed Marsannay.

"This place only got village appellation status in 1987," I said. I waved my arm to take it all in. "Before that, this was all just classed as generic Bourgogne wine. It's got aspirations; it's up and coming. There have to be good buys here. Maybe we'll get lucky. Maybe we'll find someone here."

"Take it easy," Joe counseled. "We just got here."

It made me crazy whenever he told me to take it easy. My mind was going a million miles an hour, so I knew he was right, but of course when your horse is charging down the flyway nobody wants to pull up on the reins. I stared at the vineyards. They were little parcels, one after the other, all sewn together to make one long endless runner of vines rolling south as far as the eye could see. It was a garden of vines. It was more magnificent than I had ever imagined.

"Look at this," Joe said, shaking his head. He was getting a little excited himself. "Do they do anything else *but* make wine in Burgundy?"

I clapped my hands together with a great crack and shifted up a gear. We passed a couple of other villages off to the right in rapid succession, then came upon Fixin. Joe pointed out the colorful patterned roof tile of nobility, a legacy of the duchy's days when the rich hired Flemish builders to roof their homes. That kind of thing caught his architect's eye. So did the increasing gentle curvature of the escarpment — south of Marsannay, the Côte's edge was softening, giving the vineyards an actual slope to grow up. "You said that the best vineyards are in the middle of the slope?" Joe asked.

"The middle of the band," I said. "That's where the premier crus and grand crus are. That's where they say the sweet spot lies."

With his trained eye, he appraised the slope at Fixin. "The soil is too thin on top and too rich at the bottom, right? Process of erosion. Plus the sun hits most evenly in the middle, and there's good drainage. Okay, so what are the wines like from the top of the slope and from the flats?"

He made me laugh. He wasn't even a wine guy, and in a glance he grasped an essential geological pillar of the Côte d'Or's best vineyards. "Thin and angular," I said, "and, well, thin and angular. At least generally, because up high things have trouble ripening and down low everyone lets their vines yield too much." Then I said what really weighed on my mind: "I hope Domaine X and the Aficionado come through for us."

"Take it easy," Joe said. "It'll work out."

Domaine X, as I'll call it, was a top domaine in Marsannay. The Aficionado was an old customer of mine from my retail days who was intimately acquainted with Burgundy, living part-time in an apartment that he kept in Beaune. He had an appointment with X and had offered to take me along. The idea was that X would be quick to suggest a few up-and-coming growers in his beloved but overlooked commune.

It was a pretty haphazard plan, but it was the best I had. Not a lot of domaines had returned my requests for appointments. It didn't take long to realize that every respected grower was already represented either by an importer or importers, or by an agent(s) in Burgundy or in Paris who in turn brokered the grower's wines to an American importer(s). In fact I had met with two agents in Paris the day I flew in. One was a genuinely nice man with an impossibly bad toupee; the other was drunk. Any number of appointments was possible through them. But working with agents was not where my heart lay. I wanted to make the direct connection. I wanted to find the young turks who had not yet been discovered. Who wouldn't?

But how? At that time, there were precious few publications that had anything approaching cutting-edge leads. All I had were a few confirmed appointments, the tasting with X and the Aficionado, and a list of Burgundian telephone numbers that needed calling in hopes of additional appointments. Driving down toward Fixin, I felt my horse chafe and my heart race. *Those numbers still had not been called.* Nothing was buttoned down, there was no center to hold, everything was going to go to hell in a handbasket. I glanced at Joe, the repository of knowledge *and* the linguistic talent. "We've *got* to make those calls," I blurted. Joe didn't respond verbally. His face scrunched a little, and I could feel his ease deflate as a kind of negative charge that hit my own anxiety, and the double negative created a sudden pall inside the car. Joe, I understood, feared he would spasm out again, much as he had when we first knocked at Pinard's door. He was way out of practice with French.

He sighed through his nostrils, forcibly, like a besieged bull.

A sign on the *route nationale* pointed to Fixin, now abreast of us. On a spur of the moment, I took the road into the village. Joe didn't say a word. He was hoofing the ground, preparing to charge, or something. Once in Fixin I turned left to take the road through the vineyards. This road paralleled the RN, and a sign proclaimed it to be the *Route des Grands Crus*. The grand crus! In a flush of elation that eased my anxiety, I understood that my change in course was graced by the stars, for here I was amid the vines of Burgundy and already I had stumbled upon the road to its riches. We drove through the village of Gevrey-Chambertin and then rolled right alongside the grand cru vineyards of Mazi-Chambertin, Chambertin Clos de Bèze, and, finally, Chambertin itself. They were one long swath of the most exalted vineyards I had yet seen. For me, this was big. I was like a mushroom nerd come upon a fair field of fungi. I was awestruck. Where to begin to pick among such riches?

"It's all right here," I said. I took my foot off the gas and let the car coast onto the shoulder. I turned off the engine. We both got out. I came around to Joe's side, and we leaned against the car to absorb the picture of Chambertin. It seemed somehow complete, and larger than the vineyard parcels we had just come through, but even then I realized that it really wasn't all that big (it's just about thirty-two acres). In the long-ago year of 640, a duke bequeathed much of this land to the Abbey of Bèze in hopes, it's been suggested, of receiving a pass at Saint Peter's pearly gates. The abbey's monks subsequently planted vines. Round about the same time a peasant named Bertin decided to plant vines as well, and his parcel was known as the *champ de Bertin*, or Bertin's field. This was eventually shortened, so the story goes, to Chambertin.

"Here we are," I said, rather pointlessly.

After a moment, Joe asked, "What's the word for 'tasting' again?"

I scratched my head, staring at the vines. Why was the repository of knowledge asking me? "Doesn't it rhyme with disgusting?"

"That's right," he said. "It does a little." He cleared his throat. He stood up straight. He declared to Bert's field: "*Je suis un importateur américain et je voudrais savoir s'il serait possible de venir pour une dégustation!*"

Then he shot me a look that said I'd better do nothing except voice approval. "Well done," I said.

"Thank you," he replied, and leaned back against the car.

I crossed my arms and resumed looking at Chambertin. It occurred to me to wonder how many vines it took to grow enough grapes to make one barrel of wine, the equivalent of twenty-five cases. I made a mental note to find out.

"What did you say?" I asked.

"I said I was an American importer and I wanted to know if it would be possible to come by for a tasting."

I nodded. "Think it will work?"

"I think it will," he said.

Chapter 5

FIRE BARRELS

A great pleasure of visiting the Old World is staying in one of its numerous independent hotels. These range from simple to extravagant, but what they have in common is their originality and their family ownership— a business that is often passed down for generations and usually maintained in a building erected in a bygone era. We have to look hard to find the same in America.

So what did Joe and I do? We checked into a cookie-cutter hotel managed by the vast Novotel chain on the outskirts of Beaune. It was located in a field next to the autoroute. The wine critic Robert Parker used to stay there, as did his colleague Pierre Rovani. I knew this because Pierre and I used to work together at MacArthur's before he joined Parker, and so I figured it was good enough for Joe and me. Besides, I didn't know where else to stay.

In the back of my mind, however, I kicked myself for not taking a chance and reserving a room in a small hotel inside Beaune, one full of charm and Old World ambience. There were plenty listed in the tourist guides.

But I had heard stories of tiny rooms, rickety beds, baths with handheld shower attachments, and second-rate telephones with which a dial-up Internet connection was next to impossible, so at the end of the day I went with safety and chose the Novotel chain. At the very least, I was assured of two single beds, which meant that Joe and I would not have to share. That counted for something.

My misgivings hardened upon checking in at a Novotel in Paris. It could have been a Holiday Inn or Marriott or what have you, a faceless hotel for the masses. The one in Beaune was no different, and I hated being one of the masses. In our room, I set up my new Apple laptop. Here we are, I thought cynically as I waited for the computer to warm up, next to a modern highway in a modern hotel a half a mile outside the ancient town of Beaune. It was a depressing disconnect.

Then I wrote a message to my colleagues about our progress so far, gladdened at least for that connection. Jerry, my boss, had sent me a final e-mail before I boarded the plane for Paris. "Churchill and I," he wrote, "wish you Godspeed." Jerry had a romantic sensibility about history, and I had smiled at his note. Only later, as the plane descended to De Gaulle Airport, did it occur to me that Churchill's Godspeed thing had been about D-day, and a lot of people got killed on that day.

In the morning Joe and I went down for breakfast, and the coffee was so bad that I resolved never again to stay at the Novotel. I didn't yet realize that coffee in France was only really good down south, and nowhere did it rival that found in Italy. But the Novotel's lousy coffee provided reason enough for stiff resolve, and given our alien setting, resolve seemed in order. We found ourselves surrounded by French businessmen in suits made of cuts and colors that were altogether strange to our eyes. Most of these suits were black or dark blue, but one was yellow and another was a pastel green that John Wayne would never have been caught dead in. But the guy who wore pastel green was no wimpy little Frenchman, and he was engrossed in rapidly eating a big breakfast (the buffet featured cold cuts, cheeses, yogurt, and baskets of bread, croissants, and *pain au chocolat*, as well as cereal). Joe and I were dressed for tasting in cold cellars: jeans, flannel shirts, fleece vests, and boots for the winter. We had nothing in common with these people, except, tangentially, the wine business. Moreover, we looked particularly American. The only bull's-eye missing was a baseball cap, something neither of us wore.

So we swallowed our vitamins to keep ourselves fortified (catching a cold on this trip was *not going to happen*), I pocketed my notebook, and off we went. It was another overcast, wintry day. They were seemingly all like that here in the north at this time of year, with the cloud cover low upon the land and the vegetation bare of greenery, save for conifers on the hilltops. The vineyards were brown, the vines barren, and streams of gray-white smoke pillared upward from vineyard fires where growers were getting an early start on winter pruning. One would rapidly prune a few rows, double back to gather the cuttings into neat piles, then return with a homemade wheelbarrow hammered out of a fifty-gallon oil drum, turned on its side and split open, into which the cuttings were thrown and burned. You looked down the Côte and that's what you would see: the narrow carpet of brown vineyards blanketing the gentle hillside as far as the horizon, interrupted by villages here and there, their church steeples standing tall as if to pierce the clouds, and pockmarks of fires revealed by their trails of smoke drifting up into the winter haze. It had been that way for a thousand years. Only the roughshod steel fire barrels were modern.

We began that day with an appointment with a lady in Pommard, just south of Beaune. The *route nationale* splits at that point, with the RN 74 continuing along the edge of the Saône Plain while its sibling veers into Pommard and then onto the escarpment to go by Volnay and over into a side canyon. At this split, a tall corridor of old plane trees frames the RN 74 (a remnant of a corridor that once went all the way to Paris, felled in the name of modern driving safety). When we came upon these twin rows of trees lining the road, the sight struck me as eminently French in its pleasing neatness and symmetry. Later, when I returned in the spring, the trees appeared more sinister, harboring a band of nesting crows that circled their heights and reminded me of the evil flying monkeys in *The Wizard of Oz*.

I kept my head low and they never got me.

Pommard is pretty plain as Côte d'Or villages go. Like most, it has its own *combe*, or a little watershed that cuts down through the side of the Côte. Presumably, most of these villages began life on such *combes* because of access to water. Pommard's *combe* cleaves the Côte directly behind the village and washes out literally down the middle of the village, its channel now hemmed in by twentieth-century concrete. Thus Pommard sits on an age-old pile of erosion, and its soil tends to be relatively heavy with clay and marl, making its wines broad-shouldered and structured. Upon this stalwart foundation many of Pommard's growers build wines of extracted power, as if to reinforce nature's hand (and Pommard's reputation for powerful wines). Those tannic wines can be, as the French would politely say, special. The trick is to find someone who tames the beast rather than gives it more teeth.

The *madame* we saw that morning didn't trust us at all. I got the appointment through one of the agents in Paris, and she plainly didn't trust him either. Previously, she had worked with a well-known American importer who imposed winemaking conditions upon her, which did nothing to gain confidence. In heels, wool skirt and jacket, and silk blouse, she regarded us with a fixed gaze and spoke only in response to questions. It occurred to me that maybe she came by her wariness naturally. Her house and cellar were on the main street, and if you stepped off the narrow sidewalk, you risked being killed instantly by one of the cars that, in those days before the national clampdown on speeding and drunk driving, whizzed through the little village with reckless abandon. Her world was not safe. Her wines were not too rugged or tough, but her distrust made up for that.

Afterward, outside on that little sidewalk, Joe looked left while I looked right. A car careened around the corner from Volnay and flew by, its wake washing us in a dusty wind. We had just concluded our first tasting in Burgundy.

"She was a regal lady," Joe observed. "She definitely was not walking on paws."

"Maybe it would have been better if she had been!" I said.

Joe cracked a smile and shook his head. "There was no breaking that ice," he said.

"The wines were good too," I added ruefully.

"You thought so? Good. I thought so too."

"But I think that even if I wanted to buy her wine, she wouldn't sell it to me."

"I was afraid to even ask her," Joe admitted.

We crossed the street and walked over a block or two to find André Mussy's door. I gave it a knock. His wife shouted up the stairs for him and down he came, a spry little guy hunched over a bit by age but otherwise vibrant and bubbling with enthusiasm. His first vintage was 1927, and for that reason alone I wanted to see him. He grew up farming in a preindustrial age, when horses were commonplace in the vineyards and synthetic fertilizers and chemical herbicides were only just emerging from laboratories. The moment he appeared, questions sprang to my mind. What was life like in Burgundy during the Depression and during the War; what was different about the wine in those days; and was it '45 or '49 that deserved the accolade of being a truly legendary vintage? But I didn't have the language to ask him.

"Do you have an appointment?" he asked Joe in French.

"Yes," Joe replied.

"Okay," he said, and smiled; that was good enough for him. He began talking animatedly as he handed out glasses, the old-fashioned, small brandy snifter glasses then commonly used in Burgundy, and stepped nimbly to the street. I didn't catch any of the talk, and Joe followed his light voice too intently to break to translate as we followed him outside. André was skinny. Or rather, he was bony because he was old, and he wore an old baggy sweater and an old black beret—the very caricature of a French *vigneron*—and he stepped as lightly as a cat.

Down an outside stairwell we descended into his cellar, which I remember being dark and low above our heads, and André stuck his long glass thief into barrels to pour mouthfuls of wine into our glasses. The wine was good in an old-school sense: elegant, not flashy with new oak or beefed up by overextraction, sometimes short on fruit but frequently subtly long. André would taste, then raise his slight countenance in a kind of shrug, as if to say: That's it, that's the wine, it's how it should be and if you don't like it, so what. Then without fanfare he would spit what lay on his tongue onto the gravel floor. It crossed my mind that he had spit wine onto that floor a thousand million times in his lifetime. From that thought, with crystal clarity, I realized that he knew every vintage he had made as if each were his child. While he reached into another barrel, I said to Joe, "Imagine if we knew him well enough to ask him what his very best vintage of all was, and why."

"And drink a bottle of it with him."

I nodded sincerely.

André turned and poured wine into our glasses.

"Do you want me to translate that?" Joe asked hesitantly.

"No, no—that's for us."

André looked at us, waiting, his eyes twinkling. When we refrained from speaking, he politely stuck his arching nose into his glass. In rather short order we got to the last wine, his best; it was the premier cru Les Petits Epenots. As always, he poured for us before serving himself. "This," he said with a sly grin, "*this* I drink!" He belted the wine back with aplomb and clucked at his own grandstanding. Then he led us out of the cellar. We were done.

Upstairs, he confirmed that we were importers, and confirmed that he currently worked with someone for the States. This someone was different from the importer he had worked with just a year or two earlier, which was news to me. Then he stated that one could never be too careful, and he handed me a price list. My surprise turned to ambivalence, for suddenly the price list felt like a ticket to the back of the line. But, having warmed to our presence, old André allowed as how he knew the owner of a local château who needed an importer, and he could make a quick call for us. A *château*, he repeated, his eyebrows bouncing twice, à la Groucho Marx. Joe and I laughed, and naturally we agreed.

André disappeared to make the phone call. Joe turned to me and said, "Have you heard of this château?"

"Yes," I said.

"Good or bad?"

"I don't know," I said tentatively. "But probably bad, because if it were good I probably would have heard more."

"Still," Joe said, "it's a château."

"Yes," I said. "Never dismiss a château."

We mulled this over.

"Should we feel like whores," Joe asked, "or like suckers?"

"I really don't know," I said.

In retrospect, I think André was trying to help out a buddy of his while at the same time trying to be nice to us. Joe remembers him fondly as one of the warmer personalities we met on the journey. André Mussy died several years later. He was, if memory serves from what he told us that morning, the fourteenth generation to tend the Mussy vines. When he passed away, there was no direct descendant to hand the reins to because his son had preceded him to the grave, the victim of a tractor accident. Control of the domaine went to his son-in-law, who subsequently became incapacitated by a stroke. With no one else to manage the affairs, the vineyard parcels were sold off or passed on, and today the domaine is no more.

But that morning the old man returned, dapper as ever. The château owner, André beamed, could see us right away! He saw us to the street, directed us around the corner, and wished us well.

Off we went to the château owner's office, a simple room near the post office. The visit was brief, for it quickly became clear that the wines were hard and tannic, their dryness lying like grit on our tongues long after we spit them out. As soon as we were able, we fled to Beaune.

We parked in the Place Carnot, Beaune's little main square. At the time, the whole square was a cobblestone parking lot, and you could park on its periphery or find a slot amid rows of cars on the triangular place itself. Nowadays, it's a proper *place*, with walkways, a merry-go-round, benches, grass, and plantings—a vast improvement since the advent of the automobile. Both then and now parking is free during the lunch period, although there was an interlude when a certain mayor decreed that rule obsolete, causing uproar. Today, if the ruling persists, it's not enforced.

We stepped out of the car and stared at beautiful, venerable Beaune. Small streets met the square—which is anything but square—at various angles and split off to disappear amid terrifically old buildings of two or three or sometimes four stories. Everywhere people went about their business, while here and there tourists looked about. The shops were open, the cafes busy, the town vibrant.

"We have got to check this place out," I said.

Joe rested one elbow on the roof of the car and propped the other on his open door. "Roy," he said with a weighty tone, "I came here once from Besançon. We never went through the vineyards like yesterday, we spent all of our time here, and I can tell you, this town . . . this town is so, so cool. We can't even begin to plumb the depths of how cool this ancient town is."

Me, I looked around raptly, and said: "We can try!"

As one who understood the complexities of France, Joe rubbed his beard. Then he generously waved me on to lead the way.

We window-shopped at the clothing boutiques, the many wine stores, and the drugstore promoting an anti-wrinkle cream with a great, glossy poster revealing eye-popping amounts of utterly unwrinkled female skin (I thought about the kid on the airplane again). We turned up a street, and Joe thought he recognized the *négociant*'s store under which snaked those caverns loaded with wine where he once walked in his salad days, and this pleased him immensely.

A kiosk on a pedestrian street hawked baguette sand-wiches. We bought two *jambon beurres* and a couple bot-tles of water, and continued down the street to meet a cobblestone road. We stopped on one side. They say that Paris paved over its cobblestones because the authori-ties grew tired of rabble hordes tearing up the stones and pelting the police with them during outbreaks of revolu-tionary fever. Beaune apparently suffered no such discon-tent. We looked across the cobblestone road to gaze at the remarkable Hôtel Dieu, or Hospices de Beaune, Beaune's fifteenth-century charity hospital whose solid stone walls and massive roof evoked an invincible calm.

We stared, and stuffed the sandwiches into our faces, and ate wordlessly. Joe consumed a long draught of fizzy water and burped contentedly. "I wonder how many years it took to build that hospital," he wondered aloud. "Think about all the wooden scaffolding they had, and the big pulleys and huge wooden winches and ropes they needed to hoist that stone up there back then."

I let the image fill my mind's eye. It would have been a great affair, a wondrous skeleton of wood embracing a wall of stone. It made for a very cool picture.

At the appointed hour, we met the Aficionado for coffee. We found him at his favorite cafe, the Parisien on the Petite Place de Carnot, adjacent to the main square. As directed, we entered the main *place* and simply looked up to find the figure of a Burgundian peasant painted on the cafe's dormer window. This swarthy character beckons everyone who crosses the *place* to come on in. Despite that, he and his bar have an aura of an insider's haunt, and it's easy to feel a little unworthy.

Worthy or not, we walked in. There at the zinc bar stood the Aficionado. He was radiant, boisterous, loaded with bravado and generosity. He loved wine, particularly Burgundian wine, he loved food, he loved art, he loved women, but most of all he just loved. And he wanted to be loved, but he wasn't always so lucky in that department. He shook our hands warmly and ordered us coffee in perfect French from the bartender who, of course, he knew on a first-name basis. The Aficionado was nothing if not worthy.

The Parisien's coffee did not disappoint. I should have known, I realized, for we stood in the presence of a man who understood life's pleasures. And a real pleasure it was to see the Aficionado in Beaune—a setting so perfect and fitting for this man. He sported an extravagant moustache that resembled an Old World cavalry officer's flourishing moustaches, billowing beneath the forthright nose it honored. He had spent most of a lifetime growing it. Once streaked blond, later laced gray but always flamboyant, this moustache set the Aficionado apart from the mass of men. He had spent one year of college at the Sorbonne in Paris, another rarity for an American. By 1997 he was chief of European operations for a small dot-com company. Effectively what this meant was that he flew to Paris frequently and spent time off in Beaune. He had a geek's aptitude for the details of computer technology, coupled with a businessman's grasp of fundamentals, so he did well for himself.

It was done in the service of his *raison d'être*, which was France, wine, and food, in that order (women and art jostled frequently with these three leading positions). On that day in November, he looked like a jovial million dollars, for he indulged in his business attire as he indulged in his moustache, and if the wool suit was not handmade, then it was the next best thing, and the tie that he had slipped off during the morning's train ride from Paris and pocketed was undoubtedly a noted designer's tie. Like his clothes, he took his passions seriously. In Beaune he would change into more comfortable clothes—shorts and linen shirts in summer; jeans and sweaters in winter—and continue his never-ending study of Burgundy's wines. He was a true connoisseur, which required true diligence. Thus he made a practice of visiting Burgundy's better growers to taste the current vintage, much like a critic or an importer, and often he bought. Alas, rarified bon vivant that he was, he was still subjected to the same vicissitudes that we all were.

This fact came home to me years later, after leading a tour of distributors to visit our suppliers. On that trip we were all stricken with *le gastro*. This is a twenty-four-hour stomach bug that seems to sweep through France every winter with epidemic proportions, to hear the French speak of it, knocking even the strongest man to his knees with catastrophic loss of intestinal fortitude. That winter it was supposedly especially bad—surely, commentators said, it was an exaggeration to mention it in the same breath as the 1918 influenza epidemic, but mention it they did. The viral plague caught us in Beaujolais, where we had gone to taste at Château de Lavernette and stay for lunch. The château is a magnificent manor house needing endless repair that had, centuries earlier, been a monastery for the monks of Tournus. It stands four stories tall, contains a secret chapel as well as a library full of truly ancient books, ledgers, and deeds (it became the parish seat sometime after the sixteenth century) that scholars make appointments to come and study, and its courtyard is framed on one side by an elegant stone barn. That's an oddity, because normally stables were placed in back.

One of the Lavernette forefathers, however, had been an officer in Napoleon's army. This man lost a leg in battle but lived to tell the tale thanks to his mount, so in return he built his savior a fine set of stables front and center.

The current owners, the de Boissieu family, had set a long trestle table for the eight of us in their kitchen. Bread, salad, fish, cheese, and fruit were awaiting us, along with bottles of older wines. Unfortunately, we were down to seven people, having left one at the hotel that morning, already overcome. By the time we sat for lunch, six of the seven of us had become pale, the sight of food the cause of ghastly mayhem within. Kind Bertrand de Boissieu smiled knowingly, a veteran of the ravages of *le gastro*, and showed the wobbliest of us to a toilet in a small room outside in a breezeway.

He returned to serve a six-year-old Beaujolais Blanc made from his tiny Chardonnay vineyard. The vineyard begins forty feet across the appellation border from Pouilly-Fuissé, which makes his wine the poor stepson and invariably a fine buy. This little wine was a revelation. Fragrant of apples and almonds, it was fresh, full, and elegant, finishing with lip-smacking length. And all that came from a wine that had never seen the inside of a barrel! Then he brought out a bottle of 1997 Beaujolais-Leynes, his top cuvée of Beaujolais, named after his village. The wine came from his best parcel of Gamay and was made in older barrels. Bertrand's Gamay grows in relatively heavy soils and, like Pinot Noir from Pommard, has innate strength that enables the wine to age and evolve gracefully. The Leynes was perfumed, silky-soft, and delicious—the prerequisite of any self-respecting Beaujolais. As sick as we all were, we acknowledged that these wines were splendid, and then one by one excused ourselves to go outside to that freezing toilet.

A week later I was home, having crossed the Atlantic at the same time the Aficionado went to Burgundy for a week's vacation. He had set up four days of rigorous tastings in the Côte de Nuits. I imagined him in a fine wool coat, notebook in hand and a Mont Blanc pen at the ready. I sent him an e-mail to express my hope that he would escape *le gastro*. That very day he replied:

Dear Roy,

I was thinking about the stomach virus you mentioned today as I was leaning against the inner wall of Gevrey's Clos St. Jacques [vineyard] dripping watery diarrhea out of my posterior while tearing my as yet unread *International Herald Tribune* into appropriately sized strips. By the way, it was snowing.

A.

Chapter 6

GODSPEED

The image of the dignified Aficionado forlornly tearing apart his newspaper as he squatted in the snow had not yet, fortunately, taken shape in my mind that day in the Parisien. What was taking shape was an image of rural France, fueled by the Aficionado talking about cheese. "I'm going to go see a man this afternoon," he said, "who has a herd of goats up in the *hautes côtes* behind Nuits-Saint-Georges. He makes the absolute best chevre around here." Inspired, he turned to the bartender and asked if he knew the cheeses made by the farmer in the hills behind Nuits. The bartender lit up—he was privy to the artisan cheesemaker—and they began an animated conversation in French about the guy.

"I'm going to go see him this afternoon," the Aficionado reiterated, after the bartender returned to his glassware. "Next time you come to Beaune, put aside an afternoon and I'll take you up there."

"That would be fantastic," I said.

The Aficionado lightly smacked the bar, as if to seal the deal. "So," he said, "you're going to join me for the tasting in Marsannay?"

"Yes," I said with a big smile. We confirmed the timing, and then we said our goodbyes because we actually had two appointments scheduled that afternoon.

North to Vosne-Romanée we went, where we had a tasting scheduled with a grower. He wasn't looking for representation, but he went on to recommend another grower. Maybe, we thought, the gods *were* smiling on us! We found a phone, and Joe set up a meeting with that recommended grower later in the afternoon. His French was returning; he was feeling in fine form. We ran south to Savigny-les-Beaune for our second appointment. Savigny is back up in a little hollow northwest of Beaune. It's a fairly substantial village and has, so we surmised, a wealthy inhabitant who lives in a turreted château and collects mothballed fighter jets from all over the world. They sit in his manicured yard, MIGs, Mirages, F-86s, and F-104s, a private museum dedicated to renditions of man's bird of prey. On that day, in that wonderland setting, they looked like so many big toys.

In Savigny we met with a leading grower who emerged from his house disheveled, bleary-eyed, and unshaven. He moved with care, as if a sudden step would precipitate the spins, and he looked for all the world horribly hung over. Off the cuff he said that a much more prominent and established American importer than the likes of me was coming in two weeks. The inference was that the deal was all but sewn up. He let this sink in, then shrugged and weakly expelled a mouthful of air with a quiet *phhhhh* that blew the gods' smiles right out of the sky. We went through the motions of tasting his wines and taking notes. It was surreal. It didn't help that some of the wines were very good and that I knew the other importer on a first-name basis. With relief, we went back to Vosne to taste with the recommended grower.

It was like that for the next few days. We dashed from village to village for tastings that I had scheduled from the States or that we made on the fly right there. In between appointments we managed to do things such as go to Saint Romain in the hills behind the Côte d'Or (Saint Romain was a lot closer in the *hautes côtes* than the cheese guy) and walk the ruins of an ancient castle. These ruins are perched fearfully high on a limestone cliff. From that vantage point we looked out across the forested hills and cultivated hollows of Burgundy in winter. Snow lay in the pastures, and smoke curled up from nooks and crannies where villages had sprung up long ago.

"These villages have known more centuries than I can begin to fathom," I said.

Joe looked down across the expanse. "Are you getting profound on me?" he asked.

I rolled my eyes and called him something unprintable.

We visited a grower in Morey-Saint-Denis who had stunning holdings in some of Burgundy's finest grand crus and who made just god-awful wine. He must have managed to sell it based on the pedigree alone. As we tasted, he smoked cigarettes and spoke confidently about his cellar techniques. When asked if he fined his wines (using egg whites or other fining agents to clarify the wine and take away some tannins), he replied, "Fining? *Never.*" The implication was that only amateurs did such things. But he did filter his wines; that was acceptable.

Then he spoke with dreamy fondness about his recent sexual exploits in Cambodia and Thailand, places where, he assured us, a man could exercise his libido. God only knows how we got on that conversation. He grinned rakishly and said something to Joe, causing Joe to purse his lips and nod affirmatively. "He says," Joe translated, "that a man can truly be a man in Bangkok."

"Well," I said, "we have been having problems here in France."

Joe laughed, which inspired the grower to laugh, and he slapped Joe on the back. He wasn't humble, nor was he wise; he was a macho guy who took a paternal liking to these American brothers, and in the end he led us in a beat-up vineyard truck to what he said was *the* place to have lunch, then waved a warm goodbye. This place was a large, high-ceilinged room behind a bar; it was where all the village workers ate. We had to eat because we were hungry, and tasting wine on an empty stomach is a recipe for real punishment, but we had no time. We had another appointment in twenty minutes. We rarely, it seemed, had any time to take it easy.

The room was packed with people. It was full of smoke, boisterous with noise, and at once we understood that we were no longer in Kansas. We sat at a long table with a dozen others who all knew one another and who, Joe later said, spoke French so fast that it was impossible to understand a complete sentence. I studied their faces and marveled yet again how different these people, these French, be they peasants or nobles, were from us in physical appearance. Joe and I seemed so clean, bright, and homogenized compared to the French, who sported their bold noses, dark features, and frequent crooked teeth without a trace of self-consciousness. Maybe this disparity could be linked to our Scottish heritage (Cloud used to be McLeod, although our line had been pretty thoroughly diluted down through the generations). They say that the Gauls were a blond race, a prevailing trait that disappeared once the Romans took over, hence the dark features of most French today (although in the north a rich red Celtic head of hair can be found, as well as the occasional blond). But this is a sociological can of worms; better to return to my story.

A hurried but friendly waitress came. She knew everyone except us. Joe ordered the *menu du jour* and a big bottle of fizzy water for both of us, forgoing the wine that accompanied the menu. Eventually, the first course came, a salad soaked in olive oil and vinegar and dotted with roasted giblets. I didn't know what these giblets were — gizzards or hearts or what — but Joe remembered such salads fondly and fell upon his with gusto. I dug in too, and damned if it wasn't really good, even with the pool of oil and vinegar. But then, that was why there was bread!

The second course was a leg and thigh of chicken, and green beans so cooked that they disintegrated at the touch of a fork. But the chicken was lean and tasty. We wolfed it down, mopped our plates with bread, and waited. By now we had been at the table for thirty minutes. The waitress appeared at last, a runner amid a sea of sitters, and quickly gathered our plates and asked whether we would like cheese or dessert. Coffee, of course (it went unsaid), would follow. I gasped inwardly. She stood, waiting. No way, I said to Joe, no way. We had to go. We had an appointment. We had to ask for the bill.

Joe stiffened. He leaned forward. "This is incredibly rude," he whispered. "You have no idea. This is *not* done."

"*We're already late!*" I shot back between my teeth. I tried to maintain a facade of reasoned calm, but it was cracking. The waitress—who, no doubt, was either the proprietress or her daughter—stood above us. I didn't dare look at her.

I swear I saw Joe's ears fold back. He was caught between his obsessed brother and the decorum of the French lunch break. He looked up and asked for the bill. She frowned and shot back a question, which caused everyone at the table to glance our way. Joe demurred and again asked for the bill. She turned her back and disappeared into the smoke and noise. Joe, red to the gills, pulled out his wad of francs and began slowly counting.

We paid at the bar. Outside, Joe paused. "Royboy," he said, sincerely pissed, "don't ever make me do that again."

We raced down the road to Vougeot and a well-known domaine for that post-lunch appointment. No doubt my just dessert for refusing dessert, we got blown off. It wasn't because we were late either. The guy's wife said he wasn't home, and she knew nothing about an appointment, and who were we, anyhow?

That day or the next one we returned to Gevrey-Chambertin to taste with a very kind older man. He was short, squat, and once physically quite powerful. He had an Eastern European name that stood out in Burgundy. We learned that his grandfather had come from Poland in the 1930s and in time succeeded in starting with a few small parcels of vines. He led us through a range of really fine wines, modestly answering our questions, and in the end gave us a bottle to take home. As usual, I didn't have a shot at the domaine because it already had representation, a fact that this man politely made clear at the get-go, but it was a joy to meet him and taste his wines.

We visited a passionate young *vigneron* way to the south in the Côte Chalonnaise village of Montagny. He made interesting wines, and he was clearly up and coming. The problem was that he already had representation, a fact unbeknownst to us until our arrival, in the form of one of those Parisian agents. This was becoming a discouraging refrain.

We found a half hour to go to Dijon and visit the Place de François Rude. I showed Joe the cafe where our folks had drunk Beaujolais on the square with their friends the evening in Burgundy before the accident. I knew the cafe because Mom had pointed it out to me on one of our walks. In turn, I pointed out the statue of the boy treading grapes to Joe, and then we looked at the bell tower with the mechanized man inside. We waited a few minutes, but the hour was not upon us and the bonger of the bell stayed hidden. After that, I had no more touchstones. In the silence that followed, Joe leaned back on his heels and looked around. "What do you say we get out of here?" he asked. "It's making me crazy to be here with all the ghosts." He was right; they were all around us, the ghosts. And they were mine, these Dijon phantoms. They were mine to shake one way or another, one of these days.

"They're not much in the way of company, are they?" I asked.

He grimaced. "Bad memories never are," he said. "Come on, let's go meet some new people."

We raced all over the Côte d'Or in a hallucinogenic haze induced by lack of sleep, alcohol, and anxiety at having to perform in front of strangers. We had huge swings of emotion. But one thing became clear early on, and it became our slogan: *Everyone wants to do business*. Everyone, that is, who wasn't already doing business.

We met up with the Aficionado at Domaine X and naturally X, a fine estate with superb holdings, had long been represented. But that was another wonderful tasting, and watching the Aficionado banter with the proprietor was fun, even if I couldn't understand a word they were saying at the time. They traded stories and jokes about various wines and growers, and erupted into laughter time and again. The Aficionado would pause in between the talk to taste a given wine, and if he had something good to say, he would say it, and if he did not he would not. He spit between barrels and quickly jotted down a few notes in his notebook, then deftly picked up the thread of conversation again. He was a gentleman and a good taster, and the proprietor appreciated his grace and respected his knowledge because the Aficionado got around and tasted where others did not (there are any number of cellar doors in Burgundy open to outsiders but locked to fellow growers).

The proprietor did indeed suggest several growers in Marsannay for Joe and me to visit. We were able to see two of them before leaving Burgundy, but the real harvest came after we left X's cellar. It came, as these things often do, out of the blue. On the street, Joe and I spent five minutes recounting our visits to the Aficionado. All the good growers, I said, were represented. The Aficionado expressed sympathy. He stated the obvious: that we needed to taste in the cellars of the younger generation. Then, however, he made the point that someone in a position to know this generation would be an emerging *négociant* of roughly the same generation. A *négociant* is someone who deals in wine, buying grapes or juice from growers and usually making the wine and certainly overseeing its *élevage*, or upbringing, until it's time to bottle. Typically he blends it with other wine from the same appellation to have a good quantity. Then he sells it under his own label. An emerging *négociant* would have a web of contacts among the rising growers.

The Aficionado knew of such a *négoc.* He was all the way down in Santenay, the Côte's southern anchor. We were in Marsannay, the northern anchor. The Aficionado produced a cell phone (the very thing we lacked) and offered to make the call. Joe and I glanced at each other: more driving. More driving through village after village on a little *route nationale* at breakneck speed with some French driver invariably right on our ass because our breakneck speed was never fast enough for the crazy bastard. It was never easy; it was always stressful; it was invariably an emotional rush. I looked at the Aficionado. "You don't mind calling?" I asked.

We zoomed the thirty-odd miles south to Santenay. Joe caught a catnap on the way. I envied him, for we lived on catnaps in the car, or at the hotel before dinner. I was way too wired to enjoy a solid night's sleep, and that made Joe too wired as well. In the car between appointments, however, it was different, and he conked out while I raced down the road. Asleep or not, I was happy he was here because I understood clearly now that this journey could have been one miserably lonely endeavor.

I ran through different scenarios that might arise from the meeting in Santenay. In particular, I hoped this *négociant* might lead us to a producer in Meursault, Puligny-Montrachet, or Chassagne-Montrachet, the Côte de Beaune's famous white wine communes. Those were the big blank on my small sheet of Burgundy appointments thus far.

We pulled into Santenay and spied public toilets off the main square. Public toilets, like public telephones, were a serious rarity in France, and we perceived their presence here immediately as a fine omen. After making use of them, we found the *négociant*'s office and knocked on the door. The dealer himself answered. He looked as if he was in his late thirties, as we were. He recognized us immediately as the American importers the Aficionado had sent his way. He smiled warmly, quickly shook our hands, and ushered us into his cramped office as if there were no time to spare. A phone rang, a fax printed, and off in a side room an elegant red-headed woman appeared to be arguing heatedly and precisely with someone on the telephone. With one question the dealer confirmed that I was a new importer searching for new growers. Okay, okay, okay, he said rapidly, as much to himself as anyone. He was a focused, energetic man who, it was obvious, was generously giving us five minutes of his precious time. In French he named a young grower in Pommard, a real man of the soil, he said. I handed Joe my notebook and Joe wrote the name down. The name of a grower in Volnay popped out, and Joe jotted that down. Then the dealer laughed, shrugged, and named his own brother here in Santenay, who, he admitted, was finally making good wine! Lastly, he named "the Alsacien"

Vincent Dancer in Chassagne-Montrachet, who had just made his second vintage. He said to be sure to tell Vincent to save him the three cases he had requested because he certainly wanted them.

"Phone numbers?" Joe asked.

"Of course," the dealer said. The red-headed woman abruptly finished her telephone conversation and put down the phone. "My wife," he said. He looked at her and asked if she might get the numbers for the three growers (his brother's number he recited from memory). She in turn looked at us as if we were no better than swine. In the blink of an eye, her icy glare nailed us to the cross. Later, Joe insisted that her countenance was simply the self-protective formal pose of many a French woman. Maybe so. In any event, she punched up the numbers on the telephone's computer, then waited for us to leave. We thanked the dealer. He smiled brightly, showing us out. "Tell Vincent I want my three cases!" he laughed, and shut the door.

Outside, the world had gone suddenly very quiet. There was no one on the street. There was no movement, no noise. We walked toward the main square. I glanced at the public toilets and figured they were charmed. I slapped Joe on the arm, unable to contain my glee. "Now we're cooking with gas!" I exclaimed. We had the names of four growers who had not been discovered! We stepped up our pace and on the main square the charm's spell held, for behold—*there was a public telephone!* It was unbelievable.

"Call 'em up!" I said.

Joe grinned and stepped into the booth. He paused to gather his thoughts. Once gathered, he looked at me and slid open the glass door. He declared, "Cold-calling in a business I know next to nothing about and in a language I haven't spoken in more than fifteen years while jet-lagged out of my mind is not, you know, exactly ideal."

I put my hands in my pockets. "I guess not," I said.

"I just wanted to point that out," he said.

"You did want to come, didn't you?" I asked.

"You better order a really good bottle of wine tonight with dinner," he said. He shut the door and turned to dial.

That afternoon we went to see the brother, who turned out to be the older sibling, which probably explains the dealer's scornful comment. We tried to track down the producer in Volnay but never succeeded. In the evening, we saw the man of the soil in Pommard, a tough young guy who made tough wines, proof positive once again that wine often reflects its maker as much as the site from whence it sprang. This guy had recently entered into talks with another American importer, who tried to tell him how to make his wine, which pissed him off so much that he told the importer to take a hike. He made sure I understood that. Given the tannins, I could sympathize with the importer. It struck me, however, that if you have to tell a grower how to do his job, then you made a bad choice.

But it was the Alsacien Vincent Dancer we saw first after leaving the *négociant*'s office. That he was referred as the Alsacien reflects France's deeply imbedded regional insularity, which was underscored when I learned that Dancer's family came from Burgundy, where it had lived for generations. Vincent had simply been born and raised in Alsace, and he returned to Burgundy to reclaim the vineyard parcels that his family had long rented to other growers. But he was marked by his place of birth.

Joe got him on the phone, and Vincent said we were welcome to come visit him in Chassagne-Montrachet. This was the next village north. We took the small road through the vineyards, driving in the shadow of Santenay's old windmill high on the bluff (which has since been beautifully restored). The road made a ninety-degree jog at the border separating the appellations of Santenay and Chassagne-Montrachet, skirting between Santenay's Clos de Tavannes vineyard and Chassagne's La Grande Borne ("the great boundary") vineyard, before resuming its route north along a higher contour on the Côte. Once in the Chassagne appellation, a prominent stone building on the right caught our eye. It was very old, with a remarkably high-pitched roof like the Hospices de Beaune, covered with shingles made of hewed stone. Later I would learn that this was the Abbey of Morgeot, a Cistercian abbey dating from the days when monastic orders maintained Burgundy's vines. Windowless and abandoned, it rose some distance from the road amid the vines.

We found Vincent's house on the outskirts of the village of Chassagne-Montrachet. He had a big black standard poodle on hand that day. I had this idea that poodles were prissy dogs with prissy haircuts, a notion that left me the moment we stepped out of the car. The poodle was there in a flash, just feet away. He was happy to greet us but cautious, clearly a playful dog who held his impulses in check until he could ascertain if we were friend or foe. Rarely have I ever seen a dog with such arrestingly alert eyes. Nothing got by them. I knelt and held out a hand; he stepped a foot closer. I slapped my thighs with both hands; he dropped to his elbows, the game afoot, his tail straight up. If only I had a ball! He was a really cool dog, and I was so taken by him that as the text for our initial Dancer back label I wrote:

> **Although Vincent Dancer traces his roots back to 16th-century Pommard, he exemplifies the new generation of Burgundian *vignerons*. He did a stint in an Oregon vineyard and works his vines with an open mind—and with his sidekick, a black standard poodle of remarkable intelligence. His tiny vineyards are spread among the premier crus of Pommard, Chassagne-Montrachet, and Meursault, plus he has a superb 35-year-old Meursault village vineyard. He strives to make the best wine that he can, not the most. At harvest, after selling off some grapes, he produces less than 400 heartfelt cases.**

This was one of the very first back labels that I wrote at a time when the industry standard was a generic strip label with the required legal mentions and nothing more. It turned out, however, that the poodle wasn't Vincent's. It belonged to his father. Vincent just happened to be taking care of it while his father was traveling, a fact which I didn't learn for another year. It galled me having to correct that text when it came time for Vincent to order a new run of labels.

Vincent came out of his modest house, a tall young man of twenty-five at the time. He was prematurely bald, with a prominent forehead and an honest face. He has often joked about his hair, or lack thereof. Once, relating a short history of the grand cru vineyard Montrachet, he said that it was known in previous centuries as "Mont Rachet, or bald mountain—a mountain with no hairs, like me! Because on the top of the Montrachet there are very few trees." He shook our hands and led us downstairs to his cellar. This comprised two small rooms under the house, each with a floor of gravel and each having a couple rows of barrels, none of which were double stacked. There wasn't a lot of wine here. In addition, tucked in a corner was Vincent's own private stock of bottles, which proved to be a diverse lot. He was into wine, an encouraging sign.

He passed out glasses, picked up his barrel thief, and we began tasting through the wines of 1997. He had reds and whites, scattered about the communes that I listed on his back label, with the heart of the holdings being planted to Chardonnay. These included a parcel of Perrières, Meursault's unofficial grand cru (the commune has a plethora of premier cru but not one grand cru vineyard—a reflection, it's been said, of Meursault's political impotence in the 1930s when the appellation laws were promulgated). He also had one hectare in Chassagne's La

Romanée, his largest parcel and one of that commune's best white vineyards. Then, in two years, he would reclaim two rows of the grand cru Chevalier Montrachet. Two lousy rows! Such was my immediate reaction. But the prestige of owning a piece of Chevalier is incalculable, and in the course of our conversation we learned that Vincent had penciled out a business plan based upon his family's holdings, one persuasive enough to get a loan from the bank to build his winery and launch his business. Moreover, Vincent's two rows were long enough that in productive years they gave him two full barrels, or fifty cases, of wine, each bottle of which sold for a premium.

They were promising, those '97s. The wines had been in barrel for less than two months, and the malolactic fermentation in his cold cellar had not yet started, so it was impossible to really judge the wines. The point was to see if the grower had put the wine on a good road or not. In this case the grower had, but I was already getting a sense that the man himself had a more promising future than his current crop of wine. After the '97s, Vincent opened bottles of the '96s. He admitted with evident distress that '96, a fine vintage, particularly for whites, was his first and he had fallen short. He didn't have his own bottling line and had to rely on the traveling bottling line, a common practice. You schedule a date with a private bottling service, and the big truck comes around, slides open its doors to reveal the snaking bottling line within, and, more or less presto, your wine gets bottled (mobile bottling lines came into being in the 1970s and were a great enabler to *vignerons* wanting to bottle and sell their own wine). Vincent requested a single light filtration, but the company manager bulldozed this idealistic kid into doing a sterile filtration because the manager didn't want to hear of any trouble down the road from wine undergoing secondary fermentation in the bottle. To his profound regret, Vincent acquiesced (and thenceforth that bottling company lost a customer).

The wines were stripped, and it was too bad because it was easy to imagine the quality that once existed. But Vincent's honesty made up for it. If ever a young grower was worthy of investment, here was one.

Before we left, he showed us his winery, a small building perpendicular to his house. It had been built the year before. One room was designed to receive the grapes, the other to store the bottled wine pending shipment. In the reception room were a couple of stainless steel tanks, as well as a couple new steel-encased cement tanks. The latter two were rectangular, factory-painted yellow, and stood on steel legs. They were lined with three or four inches of cement, giving them excellent insulating properties, and were used by some growers for the alcoholic fermentation of white wine. But they were not originally designed for wine. Vincent told us this with a shy smile. Without elaborating, he had us poke our heads into the front hatch of the larger tank. The cement walls within had narrow, molded racks, three to a side, perfectly spaced.

The racks were meant for coffins. The tank was a large sarcophagus: this one for six dead; the other for four.

"Many *vignerons*," he laughed, "will not use these. They are superstitious. But now the company makes them for wine as well as for coffins. One coats the cement with tartaric acid and, *voilà*, one has a perfect vessel for white wine fermentation!"

Four years later Vincent was able to return to Oregon, where he had done an internship as part of his viticultural schooling. He came with his friend and fellow grower Claude Muzard of Santenay as guests of the annual International Pinot Noir Celebration, and they proudly brought their wives. Céline, Vincent's better half, is a pistol of a woman, all five feet of her, a lawyer by training from Paris who plays a wicked game of Ping-Pong (I used to think I had talent in the game until she destroyed me). Afterward, they went for a tour of California. In the autumn, Pierre Rovani tasted the whites of 2000 in Vincent's cellar and wrote the following in *The Wine Advocate*:

> The young, talented, and inquisitive Vincent Dancer, who tremendously enjoyed the natural beauty of our national parks and the unnatural silicon-stuffed sunbathers of Venice Beach this past summer, believes that 2000 is an excellent vintage . . .

This captured Vincent well (the nature part of things, anyway). But that was the future, a great unknown to

Joe and me. What we knew that night as we pulled in the Novotel lot was that our mouths were stained black with wine and our hands were sticky with it. Outside the car the night air had become shockingly cold, but even so we moved in a somnolent zone of fatigue. Both of us could have slept at that moment. But there was no time for a nap. Our stomachs were hollow; we had to eat. The tough kid in Pommard had kept us too long, and the dinner hour was at hand.

The hotel's automatic doors slid open for us. In our room I turned on my computer to read e-mails while Joe brushed his teeth. Then he crawled onto his bed and collapsed. There was a note from the home front reporting a change for the worse in Dad's condition. Modern medicine had hit a wall, and surgeons had scheduled an operation to drill a third hole into his skull to relieve pressure. Rightly or wrongly, the procedure seemed unbelievably prehistoric.

Mom was hungry for news, so to the tune of Joe's snoring I wrote her about our day's exploits with the Aficionado, his buddy the wine dealer, and Vincent Dancer. After a few paragraphs, I was spent. As a hotshot engineer out of college, our father had reported to Admiral Rickover at Westinghouse's Bettis Atomic Power Laboratory. We had heated debates about nuclear power when I was in college. By that time, he had quit Westinghouse to move to Berkeley, where he opened a consulting firm. Mom kept the books, and the firm grew to have more than fifty employees. When the two of them came to tour Burgundy by bike, they were in the midst of retiring, having already moved to the farm in Virginia. Dad loved wine—this was something that germinated in both of us while I was in college, and when we weren't fighting about nukes, we were buying Bordeaux futures and visiting Californian wineries—and he had already mapped out a five-acre vineyard on a windy hilltop in Virginia. He would have been proud of us now. He really would have. I reached over and shook Joe's leg. "Hey," I said, "write to Mom."

He rose like a zombie. He sat at the computer and without further movement took a minute to come to his senses. I cleaned up in the bathroom, and when I emerged, Joe was typing avidly away, having read Mom's news. I took his place on that blissful bed while he wrote. I had all but let go of the world when he slapped my leg, and we walked back outside into that cold night to drive up the road to Beaune.

Each evening of our short stay in Burgundy we parked in the Place Carnot and tried a different restaurant. Being a new experience, dinner in France was an adventure. Moreover, it was the time of day when we could actually relax and let down our guard. Joe warmly embraced the rich traditions of Burgundy's culinary scene, and he was quick to point out the regional specialties on a given menu. He got his love of food from Mom, who enjoyed cooking and was very good at it. On one of the first evenings, we walked to the bistro La Ciboulette near Beaune's north gate, and Joe talked us both into starting with *oeufs en meurette.* Neither of us knew what it was, which was reason enough to order it. When the *oeufs* arrived, we studied what was for us a bizarre dish, for what American had ever heard of serving eggs poached in red wine, shallots, and thick bits of bacon as an appetizer? The eggs came floating in their own bowl of boiled wine, and you broke them so that the warm yolk melded with the red wine. You then ate the flavorful lot with a soup spoon. It was fabulous.

This time we parked on the road that circled the little *place* and walked down a dark cobblestone alley to Ma Cuisine. It was a simple bistro, said to be very Burgundian, very authentic, with a killer wine list. We arrived at ten minutes to eight, the first. A man took us to a little table near the kitchen door. He asked if we wanted an *apéro*. We ordered a couple glasses of white wine. Above us on the wall hung a big blackboard with the evening's menu, freshly written. We studied it. Our aperitifs arrived. Joe asked for *jambon persillé* to start, followed by rabbit. I took the plunge and ordered *escargots à la Bourguignonne,* followed by duck. We decided upon a bottle of red Chassagne-Montrachet because we had had such a good visit with Vincent in that village earlier in the day.

I had never had snails before in my life. But here I was in Beaune, and when in Rome. . . . I told myself this, but it only carried me so far away from what was on my mind. After a moment, I looked at Joe and said, "I really can't believe they're going to drill another goddamn hole in his head."

He flinched. "Me neither," he said. He shook his head. "I can't even imagine it."

The waiter returned with the bottle of wine and a bottle of fizzy water. He moved rapidly now because people were coming in one after the other, and he was shouting hello and simply pointing customers to tables as he opened our bottles. Then he was gone.

We watched him work. The room filled, and a general din of noise took over. We huddled closer to hear ourselves talk without being loud.

The kitchen door pushed open and a woman swung around, a plate in each hand. She wore a cook's white jacket and blue jeans; she was the chef, and she gave us a sweet smile as if to welcome us into her home before plunking down our appetizers and darting back into her kitchen. Ma Cuisine was a nice place for dinner. We felt this without having tasted anything yet but the wine.

Joe's *jambon persillé* presented itself as a thick slab cut from a loaf lying on a plate with a handful of cornichons and a jar of mustard. My snails were as you might imagine, in their shells on a molded tin plate with each oval mold filled with a sea of butter for its bobbing snail. A great scent of garlic rose from the plate.

"You know," Joe said, looking at his dish, "they poach this ham for a long time in white wine, and then chop it into these big chunks and make this terrine with garlic, shallots, parsley, and vinegar."

He cut a piece and put it into his mouth. He chewed slowly and began nodding his head enthusiastically. He cut another piece, put a little mustard on it, stabbed half a cornichon with the same fork, and handed it over. The ham was delicate, being boiled, but with the other ingredients it was a strong, earthy, surprisingly spicy mouthful whose briny flavors were made tangy with vinegar.

Then we tried the snails. They were piping hot coming out of the shell and crunchy, which freaked me out, but at the same time I realized that the texture was half the appeal. The other half was the garlicky parsley butter, which with a little bread made the crunch of the snail delectable. The snails, the ham—this was not shy, retiring stuff, this was food of gusto, and it warmed our bodies. We washed it down with the local white wine, braced with the essence of limestone soil.

"*On mange bien ici,*" Joe said.

I paused.

"One eats well here," he translated.

I smiled. I looked around the crowded restaurant. *Everything tastes good in France.*

"Dad frustrated the hell out of me," Joe said suddenly. "He'd call every so often and I would try to get him to talk to me, but he never would open up. He just wanted to see how I was doing. How the kids were. How the career was going. I'd invite him to come up to Seattle, but nothing ever came of it. I would lay out where to plant trees on the farm, but he would never do it unless it was his idea. It was never a two-way street."

I had my hands around my glass. They had had this rift for a long time, and they had never made their peace.

Now it might never be possible. This reality shrank the restaurant into a tiny space.

"He was stubborn," I said.

"He was pigheaded."

I nodded. Dad could be fairly accused of that.

"I don't know what to do with all this," Joe said.

I flinched. "Aw, Joe," I said. The waiter came. He poured us red wine, picked up the appetizer dishes, took away the empty white wineglasses. "I don't know either," I said. Dad was one of the few people I could readily talk to because he understood me. Intimately. Instinctively. Like father, like son—we had that. Joe and I were staring at a great void, but from opposite ends. It was unbearable. The kitchen door opened and this time we were ready; we turned and welcomed the chef with what must have been plaintive faces, and with her warm smile she gave us our dinner.

Chapter 7

VOLNAY

*O*ur final day in Burgundy found us in Volnay. We were there because I had read a single sentence about Domaine Joseph Voillot in a book devoted to Burgundy. Joseph Voillot was mentioned in the preface to Volnay but not profiled in the subsequent pages. I knew the profiled domaines. They were the well-known ones whose wines I had drunk Stateside, and each and every one had long ago been locked up by prominent importers. But I had never heard of Voillot, so I zeroed in on the description: "Finally, Joseph Voillot, a charming older *vigneron*, steeped in the traditions of the land, produces a near-exemplary range of Volnays and Pommards from some 10 ha. . . ." (*Ha* is short for a hectare, or 2.471 acres, making 10 hectares about 25 acres.)

I managed to find the fax number on the Internet. Someone named Jean-Pierre Charlot, identifying himself as the director of the domaine, replied to my note with a neatly handwritten fax saying that he had several

American importers but I was welcome to come taste the wines. That was good enough for me.

We found his office up in front of Volnay's small fourteenth-century church. The town of Beaune sits on the plain; just to its southwest is the village Pommard, snug on the tongue of its *combe*. You drive through Pommard and a couple of minutes later you come abreast of the village of Volnay, perched high on the flank of its hill. Farther south and back toward the plain sits the town of Meursault. Volnay is a compact little village surrounded by vines. Its streets are narrow with old houses built hard up against one another, blocking views and obscuring larger landmarks. First-time visitors driving up the hill on one of the side roads can momentarily find their sense of direction bewildered upon entering the village. The panorama opens in back of the church (the church faces uphill), where a primary road comes straight up the hill. From here on a clear day, it's possible to look across the whole width of the Saône Plain and see Mont Blanc in the Alps.

With a little sleight of hand, the sense of bewilderment can even happen to the locals. Once, returning from lunch, director Jean-Pierre noticed detour signs and temporary one-way arrows that the public works guys had put in place while they dug up a street. He followed their circuitous route through the village. Then he returned, inspired with an idea that had his broad shoulders trembling with laughter.

He took the one-way arrows from the latter half of the detour and moved them, creating a continuous circle within the village. Parking his car in front of his office, he walked down to the back of the church, where a couple of friends whom he had already called on his cell phone were waiting. One by one, locals returning from lunch drove by this small group of men who waved and smiled, because of course everyone knew each other, and then several minutes later drove by them a second time. Naturally, this flummoxed every driver. The smiles among the pedestrians turned to laughter, which didn't help, but then the victim got wind of the joke and rolled down his window to ask what was afoot. Most joined in the merriment. One didn't, and told the public works guys, and one of them came along to ask who the hell was messing with their signs. The group dispersed, and Jean-Pierre retreated to his office, savoring his small victory over the ordinariness of everyday life.

He was, and is, like that. In 2009 he came to America on a promotional tour and spent his first night at my house. He was there when I came home from the grocery store bearing food for dinner. He stood around the kitchen island with my business partner, Mike, Mike's better half, and my wife, Helen. For some reason, centered on the island was Helen's food scale. Jean-Pierre weighed a handful of almonds and explained gravely that his doctor now required him to measure his intake. This brought to mind the description of *Marc de Bourgogne* in the *Oxford Companion to Wine* (marc is the local brandy made from what's left of the grapes after they've been pressed): "A handful of *négociants* and individual estates proudly offer their own oak-aged marcs that are aromatic, rich, powerful, and the ideal conclusion to a gigantic Burgundian repast for gourmands not overly interested in extending their life span." Jean-Pierre has health issues from a lifetime of gigantic Burgundian repasts. So, I assumed, these issues had finally come to a head. This was a depressing thought. I put it aside in favor of asking him about his trip and how things were with his team, and we talked for a bit until Helen slipped a bottle of wine onto the scale. Jean-Pierre's eyes went wide. Aghast, he looked at me. But he's a terrible actor, and the joke was plainly on me.

This side of his nature was not apparent, however, the day Joe and I rang the somber silver doorbell to his office. We had parked below the church and walked around a bit looking for the office, which turned out to be in the basement of Joseph Voillot's small house. The iron latch rattled behind the door, and then Jean-Pierre appeared, two steps below us, filling the doorway. He wasn't a tall man, but he was altogether big-boned, with a chest and shoulders framed like an ox and a belly that in midlife showed a propensity for extended meals. He had a full head of hair, trimmed neatly within a quarter inch of his skull, black but speckled gray. His lips were full, his nose broad, his jowls ample, and his eyes were soulfully large and wise. He was the very picture of a stalwart Burgundian peasant (the guy painted on the dormer of the Parisien had nothing over him). Upon meeting us, he looked bored.

He invited us in. *"Attention à la tête,"* he said sleepily, indicating the stone header framing the doorway with a tap of his paw. I lowered my head with care and passed through the door. I didn't want to physically smack up against the header any more than I did figuratively, a possibility that seemed rather real in this man's presence.

We entered a small room. There was a clean rectangular table, and behind it stood racks full of the domaine's wines. To the side was a smaller table with a stack of price lists, another stack of brochures, and an adding machine, each in its own place. This room was where Jean-Pierre conducted business with his private consumers, agents, and importers.

Hidden in the next room was his little windowless office, with a big desk, computer, fax, file cabinets and bookshelves full of documents—the nerve center of the domaine, all squeezed into this basement with the ceiling pressing down six feet overhead. But it would be years before I would see that office.

Jean-Pierre stepped behind the large table and turned to face us. His head nearly touched the ceiling. He put his fingers casually into his jean pockets and regarded us for a moment. He was three times my breadth, wearing a handsome green wool sweater (in contrast to André Mussy's threadbare pullover), his hair carefully cropped down to a utilitarian burr, his tidy room bare but for the essentials—this was one fastidious grower. Joe made our introductions. On the opposite wall was a photograph, blown up to the size of a poster, showing the big man effortlessly lifting a big empty oak barrel. In the photo he wore a black work apron, and it was dirty.

He was imposing. In later years, he took to calling me Astrix, after the little Gaulish warrior in the French comics who drinks a magic potion to gain strength in the running battle with the Roman invaders. By default, he became Astrix's large, powerful, and fat sidekick, Obelix, who was fond of exclaiming *Those Romans are crazy!* That photograph came to always bring this to mind.

After fielding a couple of our questions, he explained that he was Joseph Voillot's son-in-law. He had worked with the older man since 1980 while at the same time teaching at the viticultural school in Beaune. He took over responsibility for the domaine upon Joseph's retirement two years ago in '95. He said he worked with regional American importers on the East and West Coasts but, if we were interested, the Midwest was a possibility. His quantities were tiny. Would we like to taste the '96s?

Joe smiled. Yes indeed, he said in so many words. Jean-Pierre reached behind him to pull out the wines. He lined up one bottle after another. As he opened them, he recounted a visit the day before from a Japanese importer. The man had asked Jean-Pierre which of his Volnay premier crus he made the most of, and Jean-Pierre replied that his largest holding was in the Champans vineyard, where the domaine farmed just over one hectare of vines.

The importer declared that Volnay premier cru was very popular in Japan and that he, the importer, would buy everything that Jean-Pierre could supply.

This was a sweeping statement. Jean-Pierre looked at us, and we at him. He went on to say that he asked the man if he would like to taste the wine first. No, the importer said, that was not necessary. He would buy on name and reputation alone.

Again, Jean-Pierre looked at us, and we at him.

"What did you do?" Joe asked in French.

"I thanked him and took his card," Jean-Pierre replied. "He wants to buy all my Volnay Champans. Just like that! Can you imagine?"

Yes, I could, I thought. I was dismayed. The mere idea of buying hundreds of cases of high-end Burgundy was impossible to consider. We didn't have the customers. We didn't even know if we could interest a single distributor in Burgundy. We were starting from scratch. We had no reference, no track record, nothing. What I was doing was ridiculous, a fool's errand.

"*C'est fantastique!*" Jean-Pierre spit. "Tell me why I would want to sell all of my wine to someone who doesn't care what it tastes like?"

Joe translated this for me. At the news, my demons fled, and my hopes rose.

"*C'est fou,*" Jean-Pierre added. "That's crazy. I don't do business that way."

He opened the last bottle. There were ten lined up before us. He poured the first wine.

I didn't take notes. I was too intent on talking to Jean-Pierre through Joe to bother jotting down my impressions of each wine (I've picked up that first notebook time and again while writing this, and I shake my head every time at finding not a single reference to Voillot). What struck me memorably was that each wine had its own personality. Beyond that, I'm sure the wines were difficult. They were young 1996s, tightly wound with the high level of acid the year is known for, and tannic too because in those early days Jean-Pierre continued his father-in-law's practice of fermenting with the grapes' stems, combining wood and grape tannins. They had to have been hard to taste. What likely happened is that as a young taster I gravitated toward what I could connect with, which was this large man with the thoughtful eyes. He commanded attention. Better yet, he listened to my questions and answered them carefully. I asked him about his domaine, about the various parcels he managed, and if he made one wine differently than another. I had all manner of questions.

He tended vines in four premier cru vineyards in Volnay and four in Pommard, an enviable number. Plus he had parcels in various vineyards ranked at village level that were responsible for his straight Volnay and Pommard wines, as well as parcels on the edge of the plain for his generic Bourgogne Rouge. He made the wines according to their ranking, thus all the premier crus were

made identically and they received the longest maceration and the most new barrels. But the maceration time
was restrained, and the barrel rotation ensured that the
premier crus were aged in roughly 20 to 25 percent new
wood, a modest percentage that framed the wine just so.
The aim was to let the fruit tell the tale of its origin. A lot
of winemakers say this, but Jean-Pierre meant it. Volnay
was feminine; Pommard masculine, and he didn't want
to hide or push these attributes. Within the domaine's
Volnay premier cru stable, the vineyard Frémiets was
marked by perfume and stone; Champans by its earthy
power; Caillerets by its spicy elegance. Similar distinctions can be made about his Pommard premier crus.

All of this is true today. Jean-Pierre has simply fine-
tuned the domaine's practices. But he had to do this slowly
because he had two strikes against him: He came from
outside the family, and he came from outside the village.
All eyes were upon this son-in-law from Beaune, taking
the reins of a respected Volnay domaine in 1995 from the
patriarch of a venerable local family. He began instituting
change in 1997 by taking a more organic approach in the
vineyards. With the '98 vintage, he risked picking later
than his father-in-law advised (good ripeness was hard to
find in 1998), and he began bottling the wines earlier than
had been the practice to better preserve their fruit. With
'99, he stopped using stems during the fermentation, and
he did trials involving bottling with various types and
levels of filtration and bottling without filtration. With
'00, he stopped systematic filtering of the premier crus.

All of these measures have made the wines richer, more approachable, and more individual.

Voilà, he stated quietly, when we finished tasting the last bottle (it was the Pommard Rugiens, a site whose iron red soils give its wine a commanding depth of fruit wrapped in tannins that require years to unravel). He looked at us. We looked at him. He said to Joe, "Your brother poses many good questions, and it gives me pleasure to answer them." Joe passed this along literally. Maybe he was bullshitting, but I was touched. Jean-Pierre asked if we wanted to taste the '97s from the barrel.

"You bet," I answered.

"*Avec plaisir,*" Joe translated.

"Okay," the big man replied. He handed us fresh glasses. He said that he would meet us below the church. Joe and I walked down around the church and stood before the small World War I obelisk. The names of Volnay's fallen were chiseled in the stone, protected from cars by a little wrought-iron fence anchored at each corner by an artillery shell cast in bronze. Jean-Pierre roared down beside the church in a car that seemed much too small for him. He parked in front of an elegant two-story house opposite a little restaurant, and climbed out.

He opened a pair of massive wrought-iron gates to allow us into the house's courtyard. Later I learned that this was the house of Joseph Voillot's parents, who were then still alive. During a subsequent visit I came in the autumn and met the elderly Madame Voillot as she vigorously swept this courtyard of its golden leaves.

Jean-Pierre introduced her. She paused long enough to smile and shake my hand briskly before returning to those pesky leaves. I watched her, much impressed. Jean-Pierre noticed and remarked that she was eighty-six. Mischievously, he declared, *"C'est le paradoxe français!"*

Now he led Joe and me into a side building and down a worn set of limestone steps to the cellar under the house. At the bottom, above the cellar door, was a moldy placard with ornate red lettering. It read:

LA GAIETÉ FUIRA VOS FESTINS, SI DE VOLNAY
VOUS NE SERVEZ LES VINS! 1872
(GAIETY WILL FLEE YOUR FESTIVALS IF YOU
DON'T SERVE VOLNAY'S WINES! 1872)

We entered the cellar. There were two small chambers, each filled with rows of barrels. It was a typical Burgundian cellar: dark, cramped, stone walls arching up into ceilings without a trace of paint. The floor was covered with the customary gravel, and the walls were covered with a thick, hairy black mold. It took a moment for my eyes to adjust. Then I saw that the gravel had been freshly raked, and I thought of Pinard's freshly washed floors in Sancerre. Behind the hairy black mold on the walls were little caches of label-less bottles tucked away, with moldy pelts growing over the bottles and horrid wigs dangling off them. In fact, the entire wall was nearly hidden behind a dense carpet of mold. The shelves had barely discernable signs stating the wine and vintage: Champans

Volnay

1964, Frémiets 1959, and so on. In the second chamber a cistern with a sump pump was built into the uphill wall. The cellar blocked an underground stream, and during heavy rains the water would overflow the cistern were it not for the pump. The constant flow of water explained the fierce growth of mold. With understatement, Jean-Pierre observed that he didn't have a problem with lack of humidity in this cellar.

Surprisingly, the mold turned out to be quite clean. I pulled a pinch from the wall, a mass of filaments like fine hair that, upon being rubbed between my fingers, disintegrated without trace on my skin. Once, Jean-Pierre explained, he had to get his team to strip the growth from the walls because it had grown deeper than the depth of a hand and was becoming claustrophobic.

We were in the cellar where the domaine's premier cru wines aged. Jean-Pierre picked up a glass thief and pulled the bung from a barrel. He said that the summer of '97 produced a crop of very ripe grapes whose wine inexplicably raced through their malolactic fermentation (Vincent Dancer's slow malos were something of an exception). The resulting wines were fat and fruity—an American vintage, he added. He turned to hide what was his first smile of our visit.

His craftiness in turn made me smile. We tasted the wine. It was the Volnay Frémiets, whose perfume was too young to be haunting but not too old to be heavenly. The flavors were dazzlingly full, yet light, and lingered indelibly. There was a delicious silkiness in the texture of the wine that expanded with extraordinary flavor in my mouth. I was spellbound. This, I thought, was the end of the rainbow; *this* is why Homer wrote *The Odyssey*! If this was a harbinger of what was to come. . . . It was, and it turned out that each wine was a study in site, or, to use a much bantered about word, *terroir*. Each was markedly different than the other despite being from vineyards a stone's throw away from one another in the same appellation. They were also delicious: lush, juicy, brimming with fruit. This was a function of the difference between the high-wire act of 1996 and the lushly ripe vintage of 1997, but it was also a function of the fact that Burgundian Pinot Noir hates being shoved into bottle. Prime in barrel, it's richly seductive, sensually coating the palate with flavors that have a weightless beauty, which is a neat trick (most other red wines have weight). Even the gentlest of bottlings shocks such delicacy, and it can take awhile in bottle for that wine to emerge again.

After tasting the final premier cru, Jean-Pierre turned to us. "Nice wines," I said. I meant it as a sincere endorsement of the wines, but it came out pretty lamely. He looked at Joe for the translation. Joe tried, but unsurprisingly his translation lacked the profundity that I intended. The big man stared at us. At that moment I watched our dynamic spin off kilter, but with the language barrier I didn't know how to right things. Then he shrugged and asked if we wanted to visit his Pommard cellar. Of course, we replied. He rinsed out the thief and the glasses at a wall spigot and turned off the lights.

He zoomed from Volnay to Pommard in his little car, and we followed. The domaine has a perennial problem of space, for Volnay and Pommard are historical villages and space comes at a premium. As a result, Jean-Pierre has three cellars in Volnay and one in Pommard. Aside from the one we had just visited in Volnay, he has a second one for barrel storage and a third for stock. Above the stock cellar rises a small building with two floors, each an apartment. This is where most of his harvesters stay at the end of every summer, one floor for the men and the other for the women (the spillover stay at his house in Beaune or with friends). Effectively, it's a bunkhouse, and it doesn't comply with modern labor regulations. It doesn't have the required number of bathrooms, let alone the legally mandated square footage for the number of harvesters who pile in. But his pickers come every year regardless. They have been coming an average of ten years—some as many as twenty, some much less—but it's essentially the same team, and they take holiday time to do the harvest. It's a seasonal ritual. It's a communal endeavor that binds them to the earth, and they wouldn't give it up for all the beaches at St. Tropez or the casinos at Monte Carlo. And thank God so far the labor inspectors have not been overzealous, because if they were, the result would be machine harvesting at the domaine, and for these people a connection would be cut (and the quality of the wine would be lessened).

So they come in September, this experienced team, and Jean-Pierre's wife, Isabelle, takes time off from her nursing job at the hospital to prepare whopping great meals every night with the aid of her mother and her daughters. The harvesters eat these dinners in the courtyard of Isabelle's grandparents, the same courtyard her grandmother so vigorously swept one autumn day. They sit around trestle tables and eat and drink and tell stories and sing songs. They do this for roughly seven days. In some years, the man from Lyon and the woman from Paris slip out of the bunkhouse at night to resume their annual affair in the vines, an affair looked upon tenderly by the elders in the group.

But the work is serious. They're in the vineyards at the crack of dawn each morning, the more experienced showing the newcomers how to strip out unripe grapes from the clusters, or how to shed the dried (or worse, rotten) hail-damaged grapes from one side of the otherwise healthy cluster. Burgundy has seen an increase in violent summer hailstorms of late, and Jean-Pierre's vineyards got hit in 2001 and again in 2004 (and again in 2008). Each time the storm came from the south and shredded several of his parcels with hailstones the size of Ping-Pong balls, a size I do not exaggerate here. For five minutes, the sky let loose with tremendous winds, a torrent of rain, and merciless salvos of hail. Then the tempest passed. The aftermath left mud in the streets that turned to dust for weeks afterward, and row after row of vines looking as if they had been machine-gunned.

Luckily, in '01 and in '04 the hail came at a slant and damaged only the south-facing sides of the vines and grape clusters. Luckier still, the weather subsequently was dry, so rot did not take over. Thus it was possible for Jean-Pierre's team to remove the damaged half and keep the healthy half. These they would fill their bins with and take to the truck, where the elderly Joseph Voillot himself oversaw the sorting table where the grapes were sorted a second time. On September 19, 2004, six days before the harvest, Jean-Pierre wrote me to explain how the first sorting would go. Like a coach before the big game, he was psyching himself up (the ellipses are his; the translation mine):

> The leaves of my vines are still nicely green and the maturity advances normally. There is no botrytis, no oidium, no downy mildew. Next week supposedly will have good weather so I am optimistic about the quality.
>
> The *ban de vendange* [official date the harvest can begin, set by the appellation authorities] is fixed for the 20th of September and the growers most pressed will begin then. Me, I am waiting until Saturday the 25th . . . in hopes that the good weather will continue . . .
>
> I will save much energy to watch over the sorting of the grapes.
>
> I will harvest the vines that were hailed in two passes: first the north side with the good grapes, then the south side with the hailed grapes . . . this makes a lot more work but it's necessary . . . my workers and my father-in-law are not in agreement with this because it's much more complicated, but I tell them *"merde"* because it's me who decides.

The sorting will be done in the vines and then by
eight to ten persons at the end of the rows . . . and I will
watch everything closely!

After the elder Joseph had his truck full, away it
went to the winery in Volnay. Just off the courtyard and
above the premier cru cellar, Jean-Pierre then oversaw
yet another sorting table for the final selection before the
grapes went into the press. The team worked until a break
at ten for bread, sausage, and a glass of sharp Aligoté.
They went back at it until lunch, and then again through
the afternoon. After that, they had time for a shower and
a nap. At the winery meanwhile it was nonstop. During
the night, Jean-Pierre slept on a cot in the courtyard just
outside to watch his fermentations.

We arrived in Pommard. Jean-Pierre turned his tiny
car off the main drag to follow the hemmed-in creek and
then turned onto a narrow side street. He pulled up tight
against a stone wall. Joe and I parked behind him. He
unlocked a door built into a big wooden gate, and we
went into the courtyard of the domaine's Pommard cellar. This, he explained, was where they prepared orders
and where their village wines were made, along with the
Bourgogne Rouge and Passetoutgrain (an inexpensive
wine made from Pinot Noir and Gamay). On the ground
floor he showed us the main room where the bottling line

and bundles of flattened cardboard cartons were stored. Then we went back outside and down into the cellar under the main room.

From barrel, we tasted through the '97 Bourgogne, the Volnay, and, lastly, the Pommard. Jean-Pierre looked at us, and we looked at him. He was trying to figure us out, me in particular. Within a year, he would coin the title of *Le Petit Homme Stressé* for me, and at that moment I was kind of stressed. I hadn't figured him out at all. He was a powerful Buddha of a Burgundian and a difficult read. Was he an honest man, with his heart on his sleeve? Or was he a devious peasant, playing a couple of rubes from America? I felt like a rube right then, for I had run out of questions and the absence of discourse filled the space between us. Abruptly, he motioned for us to go upstairs. He led us across the courtyard to another heavyset door, requiring another large key to unbolt, which, once opened, revealed yet another dark cellar with a gravel floor, low arched ceilings, and two small chambers laden with earthy, moldy air. Here, I saw as my eyes adjusted, lay stocks of older wines. Bottles were lined up row upon row in the arms of steel racks. In some cases the racks held less than one row; in others, two interlocking rows of label-less bottles rose to my knee or higher, their origins and vintage chalked on a little slate that hung from the rack. We were in the chambers of the mother lode.

I exchanged glances with Joe, who discreetly gave a thumbs-up. Jean-Pierre went to the far end of the second room and picked up a bottle. He faced us, standing in the middle of a phalanx of racks whose steel arms reached to the stone ceiling. He opened the bottle and poured us each a glass of wine. Of course, the wine was good—it had to be good because it was old. That was my mind-set, and with anticipation I brought the wine to my nose. But to my befuddlement, it smelled earthy and leathery, without any of the juicy fresh fruit of all those young wines from barrel. I found myself lost. I tasted what was in my glass and spit. The big man watched me. So did my brother. It was intensely uncomfortable. "What is it?" I asked.

Jean-Pierre told me, "Pommard Pézerolles 1987" or something like that. I don't remember what the wine was. It's not important. He opened another wine, and inwardly I braced myself. He poured; we tasted and spit, and he waited. I said the wine was good. He opened a third bottle. He did this quickly, forcibly. My palate was shot, but gamely I held forth my glass. I swirled, sniffed, tasted, spit, and said that the wine was good. Joe translated. Jean-Pierre's face lost interest. He leaned a massive forearm against a rack about the height of his shoulder and rested his other hand on his hip. He regarded me. He turned to Joe and said something. Joe looked as if he had just been slapped. He turned and said, "He says he knows it's good. He wants to know if you have anything useful to say."

Useful?

I am so screwed, I thought. My face burned with embarrassment. I went back to that wine. It was more aromatic than the other wines and it tasted particularly mineral, and I said as much. Joe translated. Jean-Pierre nodded. *"C'est le Volnay Frémiets,"* he said, apparently satisfied. Years later I came to understand that it wasn't me who passed the test. It was Jean-Pierre who passed, because he had made the wine properly so that a guy, however badly cornered, could nail down its constituent parts. He corked the bottle, left it on the floor, and led us out of the room. Out on the street, he indicated that we should follow him back to Volnay. He zoomed off. Joe and I hurried to our car, but the enthusiasm that had carried us here had too obviously deflated. Fortunately, if Joe thought I'd blown it, he didn't say so. What he said was, "That man is no simple farmer."

"At least we tasted the wines," I said, grasping at straws. "Maybe that puts us up a notch over that Japanese importer."

He raised his eyebrows. "I think we're about to find out," he said.

In Volnay, we descended back into Jean-Pierre's office. He gave us a price list He said that perhaps we could stay in touch.

"Okay," I said. "I will send a fax."

Joe translated.

"Okay," Jean-Pierre replied.

"In one week," I added.

"Dans une semaine," Joe said.

"Okay," Jean-Pierre said again. I took his acceptance at face value. He didn't, after all, have to give us his price list.

Domaine Joseph Voillot was our last appointment in Burgundy. I remember the start of that day well because the morning sun broke through the heavy cloud cover, a cover that had hugged the land since our arrival into Paris (already a distant day to both of us). Walking across the Novotel's parking lot, we felt the sun upon our faces, and in a rush our spirits rose. By afternoon, the gray clouds had scudded away completely. At a little after four o'clock, I said my goodbye to Jean-Pierre, and Joe and I walked around Volnay's church to catch the end of that winter day. The sun was descending rapidly now, but it was still strong on our backs and full upon the Saône Plain before us. We were done in Burgundy. This realization came over me, and I found myself immensely relieved. I had a feel for the lay of the land now. I had several promising contacts. And I had a price list from Jean-Pierre Charlot, despite having performed a face-plant before him.

"You know," Joe said, "that big guy makes some good wine."

He was stating the obvious. He knew it and I knew it, so we both laughed. We were on the square of the village's *salle de fête*, just below the church. This forms a ledge over the hillside, making a natural vantage point.

"Do you think I can recover with him?" I asked.

"I think so. He likes you."

"Good," I said. "Now I just have to learn this language."

That, too, was stating the obvious. But it wasn't so funny.

I looked out over the rolling land below and to either side. It was a wonderfully pastoral scene. What Jean-Pierre and his fellow *vignerons* had were lives anchored by communities that had long ago found their rhythms and formed their customs. It was hard not to romanticize this life, despite the presence of small-mindedness and lousy growers. Fundamentally, there was something here worthy of romance. What the good growers did deserved respect; what they produced deserved to be cherished.

"He said he could sell us some wine for the Midwest, right?" I asked.

"That's what he said."

"So, Chicago," I said, thinking aloud. "That's the only worthwhile Burgundy market in the Midwest. What do you think the chances are of doing the job for him and earning his trust so one day he'll give me the whole country for his wine?"

Joe pursed his lips. "Well, you've never been patient, but you've always been dogged. Maybe that will win out."

I looked at brother Joe, the repository of knowledge *and* nuance.

"It's even money," he shrugged and smiled.

I thought about retorting that doggedness assumed an underlying patience, but it occurred to me that true patience required serenity, and doggedness had a lot more to do with discord than serenity. I let it go. I wasn't going to win this one.

"You know what?" Joe said, all at once. "I woke up this morning in the middle of this incredible dream.

I was cataloguing the unbelievable variety—*the entire spectrum!*—of red and black fruit flavors contained in red Burgundy. It was amazing: the fresh strawberries of Haute Côtes de Beaune, the red plums of Chassagne, the black iron plums of Gevrey, the iron-only plums of Santenay—and I was on the verge of mapping out the whole friggin' Côte d'Or. But then I woke up." He shook his head, miffed that consciousness had snagged him from such a reverie. "It was a great dream," he said.

Chapter 8

THE BEAR

arly the next morning we drove to Alsace. "Ameri-
cans," the Aficionado had declared upon hearing
of our plans to go there, "are unbelievably ignorant of
Alsace. They don't even know how to pronounce it. It's
Al's Ass. Educate our countrymen about this, will you?"
We assured him that we would.

Joe was excited about this excursion because the
autoroute took us up through the Jura Mountains and
right by the old Roman city of Besançon, where he had
studied French twenty years before. In America we grew
up mostly in Pennsylvania, and when Joe's time came,
he followed the adage of "go west, young man"—to Reed
College, clear out in Oregon. Then he decided to double
back and spend his junior year at a university in France.
There, he fell for a girl. Unfortunately, she didn't fall for
him. Maybe this contributed to his heightened emotional
state as he pointed out the low-lying Jura Mountains and
the rugged limestone formations pocketing the forest.
Unbidden, I was taught the correct pronunciation of the

Doubs, a meandering river that cut through the hills and dales of the Jura, long before we came upon it. "It's *ðou*," Joe said. "The 'b' is silent—*ðou*. And the local cow's milk cheese is *com-tay* (Comté) and it's made into these big-assed wheels of cheese and it's really good."

I didn't doubt him.

"Once," he said, "I talked a couple of friends into hiking over toward the Swiss border, where the Doubs begins bubbling out of a gorge in these limestone mountains. We took a great big hunk of Comté and a couple of baguettes, and I had talked them into buying hooks and lines to fish with. Back up in that forest are these deep pools full of trout, and we cut saplings and I taught them how to fish with bits of cheese for bait. We caught four or five trout, took them back to the dorms, and fried them up for dinner. It was a big hit."

"I see," I said. "You poached the king's fish."

"We probably did," Joe admitted. "We didn't have any licenses, and even if we did, I don't know if fishing was permitted. Maybe that was why there were so many; maybe that's why they tasted so good. And I tell you all we lacked was a good Sancerre, nothing more. Now, Roy, promise me something."

"What's that?"

"We'll stop in Besançon tomorrow on the way back for a quick look around."

I agreed. Put that way, I could not very well say no.

We had only two appointments in Alsace, but they appeared worthy of the two-and-a-half-hour drive. One

was with Marc Tempé, the other with a more modern fellow. Tempé was new and unknown, but I had heard great
things about him and tasted one of his wines, a Riesling
that knocked my socks off. The more modern fellow had
a fine and well-established reputation.

Joe quieted down once we passed Besançon, and the
air grew noticeably colder the farther northeast we drove
toward Germany. Shortly before the border, we turned
due north and began our way up the Rhine River Plain.
The majestic Vosges Mountains rose all but straight up
close on our left, while the Black Forest rose way off
somewhere to our right, but the plain was dense with
mist and visibility was cut short. Compared to the high,
haughty, pine-covered Vosges, the Jura Mountains were
bush-league hills. I said as much to Joe. "One day," he
replied dryly, "you'll learn to appreciate subtlety."

The Rhine Plain itself was broad, flat, pretty much
treeless, and went on forever, or so it seemed. I searched
vainly for the river to the right, but it was below eyesight
and obscured by the foggy pall. What I knew was that a
band of vineyards lay to our left up on the rolling foothills, stitched across their flanks, and that this wine region
stretched some seventy miles long by one to two miles
wide. Here, on the plain, was where armies had roamed.
I knew this from my junior high school infatuation with
all things military.

"In 1944," I said, "there were fierce tank battles right
here."

"Oh?" Joe said.

"It was wintertime," I said. "Lots of snow and mud. It must have been miserable. They must have fought like hell too, the Germans. The Fatherland's right there." I pointed eastward.

"Did I ever tell you about the time I was invited up here by a friend from school?" Joe asked. "It was a holiday, and we hitchhiked up to his parents' house in Ribeauvillé to have dinner *en famille*. It was a typical French thing, with grandkids and grandparents and everyone in between at the table. One thing after another came out to eat, there was plenty of wine, everyone carried on bantering and joking, and I was thinking this was really neat because at last I was in the bosom of a French family. Except, and this was the weird thing, the grandmother kept giving me the evil eye. She was pretty old and had lived through the war. Maybe she was beginning to lose her marbles. I had no idea. But as the evening wore on, and as she drank more, she began to stare at me more and more, and every once in a while she would mumble something. I couldn't hear what it was, but I noticed my friend—her nephew, sitting next to her—trying to calm her down a couple of times. Then, right when the coffee was passed around, I snuck a glance to see if she was still staring at me, and she caught my eye. She had me. She raised her arm, leaned across the table, sunk her fist into the crook of her elbow, and gave me the finger!"

Joe paused, wide-eyed. He continued, "I tell you, my jaw dropped. Then she growled, *'Le sale boche!'*"

"*Le sale* what?" I asked.

"Le sale boche—the dirty German," Joe said. "She thought I was German, and she called me a dirty German! It was a real showstopper. My friend, he was furious. He stood up and ordered her to bed. I stood up and pulled out my passport to show her. She stood up and studied it. Then she apologized, handed it back, and headed for her room. I felt terrible and looked at my friend, and he relented and called her back to the table. She came back, put a hand on her nephew's shoulder, and said *les sales boches* had caused a lot of suffering. He said that *la sale grand-mère* was now causing a lot of trouble. That broke the ice, and she finally gave me a nice look."

Alsace certainly has suffered its share of warfare and occupation. Later I would stumble upon a plaque in Anne-Marie Tempé's village square commemorating the explosion and subsequent fire of a German munitions dump in 1944. It's difficult to reconcile this violence with the picture-perfect medieval villages that survive, fairy-tale-like, in the shadow of the Vosges. Ubiquitous planter boxes blaze in summer with colorful flowers in front of windows up and down the streets, and the village roof-tops proudly sport huge nests for storks—birds that, mythology has it, bring babies and symbolize birth and renewal. Maybe renewal is the key to Alsace. Or maybe there is no key; maybe Alsace just has had the bad luck to be on a border.

And then there are its people. They tend to be tall, like the Germans, and speak a native language called Alsacienne that is guttural like German rather than eloquent like French (the Rhine River isolated Alsace from Germany just as the towering Vosges isolated Alsace from France, paving the way for a unique language). Yet they often disdain the Germans and hold them responsible for any number of evils that have been perpetrated upon them over recent centuries. Once, high on the top of the Mambourg spur in the Vosges foothills, I told Marc Tempé how some growers in Burgundy worried about the radioactive fallout from the Chernobyl nuclear disaster affecting their vineyards. Marc smiled and shook his head no. He pointed toward the Rhine and Germany and, without hesitation, declared that the fallout had all stopped there—at the border!

Paradoxically, many French from other regions regard Alsace as . . . German. In terms of wine, it is true that Alsace uses those distinctively tall, Germanic bottles to house its libation, and it shares the same grapes, Riesling foremost of all. But there the similarity ends. Germany's wine tends to be far lower in alcohol and lighter, expressing elegance and tension in an intellectual way, and balanced by varying degrees of sweetness. Alsace's wines are much more powerful and bold—those from the sunnier southern end of that long band often being outright flamboyant, while those from the northern end exhibit restraint but still harness muscle that their German cousins lack the bones to carry.

Marc Tempé is fairly tall, broad-shouldered, and powerfully limbed. He sports a shaggy black mane of hair, dark eyes, high cheekbones, a serious nose, and full mouth that is quick to break out in laughter. He is forever upbeat with a wild magnetic intensity that shines through all of his wines. We felt that personality the moment we met him in Zellenberg. We had come off the autoroute just north of Colmar and turned left, and we were just about on time, which had Joe lamenting the fact that we had taken the antiseptic autoroute that ran far out on the barren plain rather than the slower local *route nationale* north up through the foothills and villages. Naturally, he had picked out that local road long before we reached Alsace, for he was the map reader, and he read maps like Tolstoy wrote novels — prodigiously.

"Maybe we can take that road tomorrow morning on the way out of here," I said.

"You got a deal," Joe said. "Now turn right here. Zellenberg's just after Riquewihr."

Riquewihr is one of those beautifully preserved medieval walled villages, a jewel of the Vosges. Zellenberg, next door, is walled as well but is a much smaller village, and it grows up the side of a rather small but distinct hill. On top is where the original hermitage perched in the Dark Ages (*Zell* refers to monasteries or abbeys). Now on top is the square where the German ammo dump blew up.

We drove up the saddle of the hill and entered through the big *porte*. The historic record has the first fortification going up in 1252, when a lord built a castle on the hilltop. We continued halfway up through the village to the first little square. There was an old public water fountain there, and room for about four cars. A second street began at the side of this little square and ran up to the top of the hill parallel with the main street to connect to the big square, and *voilà*, this rectangle was the *vieille village* of little Zellenberg.

We parked in front of the little fountain. I left the car in gear and set the brake so our trusty Renault wouldn't betray us and roll away. To our left was a pair of large wooden stable doors on the ground floor of an old two-story timbered house, its main beams exposed in the manner of Elizabethan architecture and bent with age. The second floor was the residence; the ground floor housed the stables and cellar. This, Marc would tell us, was a typical Alsace dwelling from an agricultural past. On one stable door hung a modest sign announcing the cellar of Domaine Marc Tempé. We knocked on that door.

"*Oui?*" a powerful voice hollered from deep within.

"*Marc Tempé?*" Joe yelled in return.

"*Oui, c'est moi!*"

"*C'est les frères Cloud pour notre rendezvous!*"

Silence followed. We waited. We continued to wait. The more we waited, the more conspicuous we felt, having bellowed our arrival before God and the whole village. If this were a slapstick movie, I thought, this would be the moment—just before the door opened—when the Renault rolled backward down the street behind us. I stole a glance over my shoulder. Then the latch clanged, the big old wood door opened, and there stood Marc Tempé. Calmly, he sized us up. He smiled unabashedly and said, as much to himself as to us, "*Les frères Cloud.*" He pronounced Cloud as *Klew'd*. His voice was as deep as his hair was black.

"*Entrez!*"

He threw back the door, and in we squeezed into a narrow path amid pallets of wine, a battered forklift, tanks used for settling his wine before bottling, and a big wine press, all stuffed in this dark stable whose high ceiling was supported by gnarled timbers. On the seat of the old forklift lay a giant gray cat. Her eyes had languidly opened to see who was the cause of all the commotion, and they were pure, striking chartreuse, those eyes. My hand was halfway to her head when Marc barked, "*Attention!*"

"Don't do that," he said. "She will eat your hand."

Joe translated. I withdrew my hand. Marc looked at me and then to Joe, and observed, "You are here to help him."

"Yes," Joe replied.

"Ah," Marc said. "So, next year, will you come with him, or will he speak French?"

"Good question," Joe said. "I guess we'll see!"

Marc smiled. "Well," he said, "he still has his hand."

At this, he glanced at the cat and chuckled. Then he excused himself and brushed by us to walk down a sagging wood staircase in back of the stable.

"What did he say?" I asked.

Joe gave me one of his meaningful looks. "He says you have one foot in and be careful not to let the door slam on it."

"Wonderful," I replied.

We went to the top of the staircase. About five feet below was a narrow stone cellar of indeterminate age. Against the walls were huge weathered *foudres*, or wood casks of various sizes lying on their sides upon great wood girders. Some of the casks rose about five feet tall off the girders, others closer to six or seven feet. They were old too, these monstrosities, wrapped with long bands of steel to hold their slab-sided selves in place. All had transparent plastic air locks sprouting out of their tops, filled with water, and sporadically a cask would erupt and bubbles of gas would gurgle resoundingly out of the lock like an enormous, satisfying fart.

"Had Mary Shelley been here," I whispered to Joe after the third blast, "she would have included this cellar in the Frankenstein laboratory!"

Joe's eyes brightened. "What a missed opportunity," he whispered back. "Frankenstein could have been loaded with flatulence!"

The far stone wall glistened with drops of water. Our breath was visible in the air. The floor at the base of the sagging stairway was paved with ancient cobblestones that had settled into drunkenly uneven patterns over the centuries. This cellar stepped down into another cellar, equally narrow and wet and stuffed with *foudres*. It stepped down because it followed the wall going down the hill—the wall was the original fortified wall, a fact which Marc pointed out to me at a later time. He maintained that it and the stone floor, laid directly on the ground, kept his cellar humid and at a steady temperature, which permitted his wines to ferment slowly over the autumn, winter, spring, summer, and to repeat the cycle if need be—which increasingly, the more experienced Marc became, the more he let happen. Leaving white wine on its lees in *foudre* for two years is not something ordinarily done anywhere (nor is it part of any business plan an accountant would readily sign off on). Many a New World winemaker would scoff at this; he or she would say that Marc's fermentations were stuck because he relied on weak indigenous yeast rather than using yeast carefully cultured in a laboratory. Marc in turn would roll his eyes and ask if the freshly educated winemaker wanted to make Coke or make wine.

This would sincerely frost the New World winemaker, were he present. Be that as it may, the fact is that most domaines in Alsace harvest high yields by machine, ferment with laboratory yeast in stainless steel tanks, bottle the wine early in the spring with a nice dollop of residual sugar, and rush the wine to market thoroughly sulfured and filtered. That, for Marc, is Coca-Cola, an industrial product defined above all by uniformity.

No doubt there's middle ground between our New World winemaker and Marc. But to Marc, uniformity, being the polar opposite of individuality, is everything he abhors. The logical extension of uniformity is that it has no respect for *terroir*. The heart and soul of the French appellation laws is the concept of sanctity of site. It's a simple and brilliant concept. Jean-Pierre, for example, doesn't make Pinot Noir; he makes Volnay and Pommard. Without this guiding principle, wine can quickly become just another beverage, one unhinged from nature and bereft of spirit.

Below us, Marc found a carton of wineglasses in a corner. He went to a *foudre*, pulled the wood plug from the wood spigot, and wine pissed into the three glasses in his hand. He held them out to us, and we descended the saggy stairs. "This year's wine," he said, "this we drink!" He drained his glass in a fell swoop and swirled the wine vigorously in his mouth, then swallowed and smacked his lips. I could have sworn he purred. Then he turned his dense dark eyebrows full upon us.

The wine was milky, rich with fermentation odors, fat with sugar, and impossible to judge without experience. Except clearly there was immense fruit in the making, underpinned by a fine cut of acid in a finish that had already begun to detail a stony length.

"Whoa," I said, "this has terrific fruit and minerality!" (After Voillot's cellar, there was no way I would ever say a wine was merely good again, but right then it was easy to say something more grandiose.)

"Riesling Mambourg Grand Cru," said Marc. He didn't pronounce it Riesling. He said *Ree-zz-lingg*. Mambourg, he added for Joe to translate, always has power. For him, site trumped variety.

"Come," he said, "I'll show you the vineyards."

We walked up the rickety stairs and down the narrow path through the cramped quarters of that cellar. The lion of a cat had let her eyelids fall shut, and she lay curled contently in the forklift seat. I hesitated a moment to look at her. Behind me, Marc issued another warning, but this time in a whisper, chuckling, *"Attention, Monsieur Klew'd."*

———◦⌒⌒⌒◦———

The Renault had not rolled away. That stroke of luck inspired me to hand the keys over to the native. He drove us down the main road past Riquewihr, and soon thereafter we cut up the back side of a prominent foothill. This was Mambourg, a spur jutting out onto the Rhine Plain. The road he took up was impossibly narrow, bordered by deep, car-killing culverts for runoff and stone retaining walls that held back row upon row of vines trellised three times as tall as in Burgundy. He drove our little Renault at breakneck speed up that steep hillside, stopping at an intersection here and there, revving the engine to keep from rolling backward, and whipping around blind corners.

We reached the plateau and Marc pulled off onto a dirt road. Mercifully, he slowed down, for the road was a minefield of hills and dales in miniature. Then he stopped. We pushed open our doors against a wind that blew without remorse. It was immediate, relentless, fiercely cold, and it instantly flew up my pants and down my neck. "Man alive!" Joe gasped. "The north wind," Marc observed, perforce speaking loudly. "It always blows up here. I almost never," he added, "have to worry about mildew in this vineyard." He pointed to a small parcel and said, "Rodelsberg." It was a *lieu-ðit*, a place-name—in this case, the name of the vineyard. Every piece of ground in France has a name, and this bit on top of this windswept plateau was named Rodelsberg. I asked about the word's origin, and Marc explained that *berg* referred to a village and *Roðel* to rocks, so it meant a village of rocks. The vineyard borders were composed of piles of rocks, now with brush growing over them. This was the debris from the ground dug up by his father in the 1950s, before he put the vines in.

The soil was red with iron oxides and infused with limestone. Raked by the north wind, the climate was intensely dry up here, almost Mediterranean. In fact, Marc said (and this astonished me), in terms of rainfall, Colmar in Alsace is the second driest city in France after Perpignan on the Mediterranean coast next to Spain. He tended Gewurztraminer here, along with Pinot Gris, and in this harsh *terroir* the vines naturally gave low yields. He thought about one day making this wine in small Burgundy barrels. The idea rang alarm bells in my mind and made me think of Vincent Pinard in Sancerre, who masked the crisp fruit of his Sauvignon with oak. But luscious Gewurztraminer and Pinot Gris are not high-tensile Sauvignon, and some years later, when Marc did indeed begin making his Rodelsberg wines in older—older being key—barrels purchased from a fellow biodynamic viticuturalist in Puligny-Montrachet, the results were spectacular.

The principles of biodynamic viticulture are vital to Marc. His measure of success is the extent to which his wines express the essence of nature. Of course, just about every winemaker in the world could lay claim to that. But for Marc, this creed defines him.

Biodynamic viticulture is organic farming that stresses soil fertility and vine health. It's certainly a plus that such vineyards are safe for the kids and dog to run around in, but there's more involved, as the Greek roots of the words indicate (*bios*, life, and *dynamis*, energy). The idea is to harness the power of nature and make the vines so healthy naturally that disease is held at bay and the grapes are produced at peak performance. The soil is tilled frequently with manure and compost, and the vines are sprayed with diluted vegetable and mineral extracts. Quartz is a big one, for this crystal holds light, which is energy, and in the spring the vines search for light to flower and fruit, so an application of quartz on the leaves helps them. That's the idea, anyway, and it's easy to scoff at. But the idea goes back to a traditional understanding of the solar forces that control the seasons, and the practice is to work with such forces. When the moon is in close rotation to the earth, for example, one must be on guard against fungus and mildew pressures because the moon's gravity draws water upward (a demonstrable fact in a school of thought that frequently lacks such facts).

Biodynamic farming is the sexy show on the block right now. Detractors say it is at best a fad and at worst a religious sect of fanatics who pray at an altar of meaningless cosmic forces. Proponents contend that it is the most dynamic alternative to conventional farming since the advent of modern agrochemicals and fertilizers defined . . . convention. The politics defy easy resolution. For me, there is a simple truth: The serious biodynamic *vignerons* really do care, so they tend to pay attention to the details, and it is those details that go into making really good wine.

An accompanying truth is that serious biodynamic and organic *vignerons* by definition give precedence to their vineyard work over their cellar work, and this is so both because the distinctions between them and "conventional winemakers" are most evident in the vineyard, and because traditionally a *vigneron* — one who is both grower and maker — has always been a farmer first and a maker second. Without good grapes, good wine is impossible, regardless of all the fancy ingredients and manipulating technologies available in a modern cellar. Unfortunately, modern wine schooling, particularly in the New World, stresses those cellar technologies, and encourages the great divide between "winemaker" and "vineyard manager."

Another truth is that established biodynamic vineyards in France tend to produce grapes with higher levels of acidity than conventionally farmed vineyards. These grapes foster higher-toned aromatics and clearer delineation in the wine, and a slower, longer evolution in the bottle. Since the soil is frequently tilled, the roots grow deep rather than wide, and since the soil and vines are fertile, the roots grow with vigor. The deeper the roots grow into the mineral subsoil, the higher the acid in the fruit and, frequently, the more pronounced the taste of stone in the wine.

Back up on Rodelsberg, Marc spoke about how the grapes here even gave him tannin in the white wine. The grape skins hardened against the wind, and the pulp was tight and compressed because the *terroir* was so parsimonious (he always spoke in terms of *terroir*—from *terre*, of the earth, and "ecosystem" would be the rough translation—but it wasn't just the dry rocky soil, or the constant wind, or the hot summer sun on top of this plateau; it was everything in combination). So while the wine had intensely rich flavors, it finished with a drying hint of tannin (think of black tea, which is loaded with tannin and leaves a chalky dryness in the mouth). With what I came to know as characteristic physicality, he emphasized this by pressing his tongue against the roof of his mouth, then snapping it off with an *ick* sound.

We followed him back into the shelter of the car and proceeded down the rutted road. Ahead was a memorial to the French Resistance, the tricolor flag whipping high in the wind. Ahead of this, on the point of the Mambourg spur, stood a second memorial dedicated to the American divisions that liberated Alsace in 1944. We stopped there near the stars and stripes high on its pole, where normally a fine view is afforded of the Black Forest far across the plain. On that overcast day, however, we stepped out into the wicked wind and saw little but felt much. It was the damnedest wind I had ever experienced up till then.

Marc took note of me huddling inside my coat. The situation was comical, and he and I laughed together. Then he smacked his palms together and declared in a booming voice that the story of Alsace is the story of faults. He launched off on a geology lesson, which, he added, would become clear once we drove down into the cul-de-sac just below. The hilltop we stood on formed one side of the sac, and in the little valley below was the village of Sigolsheim, where Marc grew up. After telling us about rocks and seismic shifts, Marc explained how Sigolsheim was destroyed in 1944. (*Tank battles!* I thought.) The Yanks were up here on the Mambourg spur; the Krauts held Sigolsheim down below. The fighting had become intensely bitter now that it had all but reached the German border. The Americans looked down at all that potential house-to-house fighting and said forget about it, and called in the artillery. They flattened everything save the old Roman church. After the war, the U.S. army put up temporary housing, but it wasn't until 1954 that Marc's parents were able to move out of their prefab building and into a real house in the rebuilt village.

Imagine: nine years in a temporary Quonset hut, waiting for your life to be rebuilt.

We drove partway down into the Mambourg grand cru vineyard on the side of the hill and got out to look at one of his tiny parcels of Gewurztraminer, this one planted in the early 1930s. Now the doors sprang open easily, and I stood outside the car for a moment to take solace in the fact that we were suddenly below that evil banshee of a wind. The parcel was named *Steinigerweg*, referring to a stony path that once traversed its vines. In years favoring late-harvest wines, Marc makes a world-class dessert wine from *sélection des grains nobles*, or special selection of botry-tised grapes, that he calls "S" from this parcel. Botrytis is the good, or noble, rot that concentrates sugars. It's a prerequisite for great sweet wine, and a little can be har-nessed effectively for lushly ripe white table wines.

Farther down the road but higher on the flank was Marc's parcel of Riesling, a rare grape on this particu-lar grand cru hillside. He talked about wanting to hire a horse to plow these rows. He liked the idea of a horse, but there were practical considerations for a small parcel as well. Unlike a tractor, a horse could squeeze through the narrowly spaced old rows; horses don't roll over on steep hillsides; and horses don't compact the soil nearly as much as tractors do. Shortly after the millennium, Marc found his horse and rented it once a year thereafter.

The three of us descended to the cul-de-sac. It was occupied by vineyards at the base of the hill, and by Sigolsheim and a neighboring village, all embraced on three sides by the Vosges foothills. It was in those low vineyards that Marc's lesson did indeed become clear. Eons ago, the Vosges and Germany's Black Forest were one range. Then a great geological upheaval occurred, splitting the range and creating a vast plain, which came to house the Rhine River. The Mambourg spur juts far out across this plain. On the steep southern flank of the spur grows the Mambourg vineyard, one of the warmest grand cru vineyards in Alsace. Adjacent to this vineyard, just to the west on the flank, grows the Furstentum grand cru. Then there's a little geological fault in the form of a narrow ravine that cuts the spur off from the body of the foothills. Afterward comes the Schlossberg grand cru, which appears to belong to the Mambourg spur except for the narrow ravine. You see all of this from Marc's Priegel vineyard at the base of Furstentum. Schlossberg grows in granite soils while Furstentum and Mambourg grow in limestone soils. On top of the plateau Rodelsberg inhabits its arid world, whereas Priegel, at the base of the spur, usually gets botrytis because of all the humidity down there, and this really concentrates the white grapes, giving him his best Pinot Blanc. He went on to say that the Vosges protect Alsace from rain, which is a good thing because vines don't much like rain and that's why, he added, Bordeaux is such a second-rate place to grow grapes. He was joking, but not entirely.

We clambered into the car a final time and roared back to Zellenberg. In the cellar, squeezing by the forklift, I saw that the huge cat had disappeared. I wondered if the mice in this cellar were as proportionally huge. Then I figured that the mice had long since all been eaten.

Marc dug around various pallets of wine and yanked out bottles here and put them under his arm. We followed him back outside and up the street a couple of houses to where he lived (the house above his cellar belonged to his mother-in-law). We passed through a wood gate and onto a cobblestone driveway that came down around behind a street-front house. The driveway was wet, with a few scraggily trees stained black by winter rain to one side and a stack of pallets to the other. In the middle was a make-shift ramp made from a piece of plywood and a cinder-block. There was sudden yell, like an American boy might yell *Geronimo!* This was followed by the excited barking of a big dog. Then a kid came flying into view on a bicycle with a yellow Labrador bounding behind. He popped a wheelie over the ramp, caught a good amount of air, and skidded out in a wild fishhook. "*Wow!*" he exclaimed with a piercing French accent. He gave us a great grin. The Lab stood to put his front paws on the boy's back, his tail thrashing about like a huge sausage.

"Simon!" (*See-mon!*) Marc said to his son, and went on to say what I took to be the equivalent of take it easy. Paco the dog turned his attention to us, and Marc definitely told him to take it easy. We continued up the driveway, Marc leading, Simon behind yelling to Paco to stay with him, and in the middle walked Joe, him-self the father of two, marveling at the opportunity the boy had to hurt himself. Pensively, he shook his head. "I can't stand how parents these days control every minute of their kids' lives," he said to me. "I was adamant that Kaitlin and Christopher have the freedom to live and explore—you know, just like we had growing up in the country. But every time I see something like that I cringe and cross my fingers."

I didn't have kids, but it was easy enough to imagine.

We passed under an enclosed bridge connecting the house on the street to a similar building behind. This second building looked like it also once housed a stable on the ground floor. We climbed up a stone staircase to the bridge. At the landing, Marc turned to us and announced, *"La maison."* He said this as if presenting a castle, and he smiled at his own airs.

We hung our coats on a rack in the vestibule and walked down the timbered bridge to another wood door, which opened to the Tempés' apartment. It was an old attic, with beams held together by mortise and tenon, and wide floorboards that had once been varnished but never painted. Somewhere along the line the attic had been converted into a cozy apartment. Heat radiated from a wood-burning stove in the small living room, one wall of which was covered with bookcases filled with books, CDs, a stereo. There was a narrow kitchen long enough to hold a trestle table, and off this were a couple of small bedrooms. There was, in addition, an open wood staircase running up along the beams at one end of the kitchen that led to what was now the attic, entered by a trapdoor.

But I didn't notice all the details right away. What I saw first, upon sitting at the table and glancing up at the attic staircase, were more cats: two of them, each squatting on its own step like a bookend, high upon that staircase. They were dark tabbies, with thick, jet-black tiger stripes running through their dense fur that reminded me of the tiger suits the Green Berets wore in Vietnam. They were big, these cats. All the cats in Alsace, it was clear, were big. These two lions sat on their perches and stared down at me with implacable eyes. It occurred to me, what with all the trials and tribulations of Alsace's tumultuous past, that maybe the local breed had acquired a savage warrior instinct.

Now, I thought, I knew how Joe felt when the grandmother stared at him.

I looked at Marc and guardedly pointed to the cats. Again the warm chuckle rumbled forth from his abdomen. I needn't worry, he told Joe; these cats were friendly. "That other one," he added, shaking his head, "she's special."

He gave us each a glass and bowl, and joined us at the table. From the box, he pulled out the first of the '96s.

It was a bottle of Sylvaner. Usually this is an innocuous, acid wine, often sweet to hide the acid. Marc's was ripe and stony, its minerality intensely appetizing. It was the best Sylvaner I'd ever had. In fact, later that year I brought some into the States only to find that convincing people to buy the wine was impossible, which all but drove me to distraction. In those days if a white wine in America wasn't Chardonnay, Sauvignon Blanc, or Pinot Grigio, it already had one foot in the grave. Fortunately, things have progressed since then.

The second wine was his Pinot Blanc Zellenberg, a wine made from parcels on the Zellenberg hillsides. In Alsace, wines are named after the grape variety as is done in much of the New World, with the site name appended. This practice originated after the First World War, when the regional syndicate came up with the idea of varietal naming as a marketing strategy to help the growers sell their wares after the devastations of the war and the phylloxera epidemic. Marc's Pinot Blanc was a delicious wine, perfumed and plump with white fruits.

Then came the Pinot Blanc from the tiny Priegel vineyard. I had just come from walking down a row of Marc's vines there, and the memory of the soft and spongy soil underfoot was at hand. His neighbor's parcel one mere row over hadn't been tilled in ages, and walking on that soil was like walking on rock (which at once had me thinking of Thierry Merlin's Chêne Marchand parcel from the preceding week). Marc had kicked aside a tuft of grass in his row and scooped up a handful of dirt. He had us smell the rich loam, and said that was what live soil smelled like. So I was curious about the wine. In the glass, it smelled simultaneously of white flowers and stones, and in the mouth it was rich and textured, bordering on exotic. It ended with terrific length.

Then the door opened, and in walked Marc's wife, Anne-Marie. She had terrific length herself. Thick red hair flowed down her back to fall below her waist, and she walked on a regal pair of long legs. She was slim, quiet, nearly as tall as Marc but without any of his burly qualities (she calls him her bear), and as she put her hands on his shoulders their bond was plain to see.

She and the ninja cats clearly had a bond too. At her entrance they stood, stretched, meowed one after the other like twins, then ran down that rustic wood staircase with surprising agility—for it wasn't, I saw with a pang of disappointment, so much muscle as it was a certain corpulence that created their bulk. Onto the counter they sprang to purr and coo at her touch.

We made our introductions. She spoke English, and I learned that the girl in the photo on the wall playing a Shakespearean character was indeed her daughter Marie. She was a beautiful girl, and a couple of years later I would find her a home in Napa Valley with a winemaking family for a month so she could improve her English. At the time, she was a teenager, and the mother of the Napa family was a little in awe of Marie because her legs came up to *here* (she told me this on the phone, and I could imagine her hand raised high in the air) and she wore these tiny shorts, and she went off on an overnight camping trip with the Skupny boy!

No one ever really learned what happened on that camping outing. But at least once, after Marie's return, the phone rang in the dead of night. Marc picked it up in a fog to hear the plaintive voice of the Skupny boy asking—in that confounded English that Marc never could understand—for Marie. The boy's passion had blinded him to the nine-hour time difference between California and France. Marc rolled his eyes and told the boy in French to call back later.

Marc put the Priegel aside and pulled out a bottle of Riesling Zellenberg. Anne-Marie raised her eyebrows. *"Moi, j'adore ce vin,"* she said. Me, I adored everything — Anne-Marie, Marc, my brother, even those fat commando cats — and I really wanted to adore the wine too, so when I found that it was in fact delicious, I was overjoyed. Neither severe nor cloying, the wine tasted of the essence of spring flowers and crunchy green apples. Like the Sylvaner, Marc got all this flavor from beautifully ripe grapes that were handpicked and had no need of chapitalization (the common practice of adding sugar during fermentation to boost alcohol, a response to the harvesting of green or barely ripe fruit). Moreover, both wines had fermented dry and had no residual sugar to pump up their flavors.

Next Marc pulled out a Riesling made from the Burgreben vineyard, and so on it went. With each wine he told us about the soil, whether it was limestone or granite, and whether that in turn was sandy, gravelly, marked by clay, or what have you. Then he would tell us the age of the vines and in what direction the vineyard tilted to face the sun. These, for him, were the defining factors that gave meaning to wine. After that, it was just up to him to keep the vines carefully pruned and healthy, harvest at the right time, and let the fermentation play out properly.

Marc was the first to smile and joke about this or that, but when it came to the wine, he was serious and quite sure, and there was no arrogance about his confidence. Later when we took him on a tour of the States, he so impressed distributor teams with his passion as he led them through a tasting of his wines that it didn't matter if he spoke no English. The translation never did justice to his emotion, but then, it didn't need to.

I was taken by him that day in November with Joe, and I returned to the States convinced that I'd found the most promising new *vigneron* on the Alsace block. I tried to peddle Marc's Sylvaner with little success, but that only fired me up more. I told everyone I knew in the wine trade about the Bear of Alsace, including of course my old colleague and now wine critic Pierre Rovani. From the first, I shied away from taking advantage of our friendship, but Alsace was one of the regions Pierre reviewed for Parker, so I could rightly ask him to visit the domaine. When he agreed, I was ecstatic: Domaine Tempé would be reviewed by *The Wine Advocate*! This was in the early days of our new careers when innocence shined brightly, something that Pierre perceived better than I. All I understood was that Pierre would be bowled over by Marc's wines and be every bit as captivated and inspired as me. God would tap him on the shoulder; he would see the light; he would have the knowledge.

I marked the date of his benediction on my calendar.

The morning following Pierre's fateful meeting, I went straight to my fax machine in my home office. Sure enough, there was a page waiting with Anne-Marie's familiar handwriting. Beaming, I snatched it up. Seconds later, had someone poured a bucket of ice water on me, the effects would not have equaled the shock of her words:

Bonjour, Roy,

How could you?!!
     This man, M. ROVANI, is HORRIBLE! He came
to our house to finish tasting and was totally rude.
When he left, Marc told me he wanted to hit him. He is
a jerk, an asshole, a complete fucker!
     He will never be invited back.

Anne-Marie

PS: He stole our dog!

I had never heard her use such language. For the life
of me, I could not imagine her doing so. Something awful
must have happened to make her talk like that. What the
hell had Rovani done? And the business about the dog,
that was completely crazy.
     Helen was reading the paper in the kitchen, a cup of
coffee at hand. Wordlessly, I showed her the letter. My
hand was shaking. She read it and burst out laughing.
     "Pierre!" she exclaimed.
     "Pierre?" I repeated.
     "Pierre!" she said, and laughed again. "He stole their
dog! That's really funny!"
     Oh, the cruelty of it all. Pierre had put Anne-Marie
up to it. He had told her what to write. Not for the first
time in my life did something take me back to a day in
my childhood, when I suddenly realized that the word

"pedestrian" meant something completely different from "Presbyterian"—that Presbyterians did not, in fact, enjoy the special street crossing rights those yellow street signs had made me think they did with such bewilderment.

"If he wasn't twice my size," I swore, "I'd hang him from a nail by his underwear."

From the beginning, Marc made wines layered with depth, grace, and finesse. Often, he hit home runs. But sometimes he'd miss altogether. The safe middle ground was a desperate dark corridor for him. His entire batch of the '97 Pinot Gris Zellenberg turned into sparkling wine when it underwent secondary fermentation in bottle. It was good, as sparkling wine goes, but that didn't help the situation much. He hated filtration because it stripped the wine, and he hated sulfur as a necessary evil because it really did shut down the wine. So he always went light, if at all, with filtering and light with his sulfur additions (relying equally on the natural carbon dioxide to protect the wine rather than voiding this gas). When you leave plenty of food—flavor would be another way of looking at it—in a wine and don't really suppress the remaining yeast, your wines can be ticking time bombs. And plenty of food is no overstatement. Frequently, his nonfiltered wines had great gobs of gunk floating in them.

People freak out about great gobs of gunk in white wine. But they don't freak out about piles of pulp in natural fruit juice. What they fail to consider is that wine is fruit juice, and alcohol in wine has the salutary effect of killing bacteria. Orange juice can't lay claim to such protection.

Marc knew the risks as well as anyone. For years prior to making wine, he was a lab technician with the *appellation contrôllée* governing body. Later he became a vineyard expert for the same body and helped select vineyards for grand cru status, but he never lost the background in chemistry. He chose to take the risk. Normally he won the bet, and the public drank stunningly delicious, benchmark wines. But now and again bottles went south and he lost the gamble, and that wonderfully amorphous thing known as "the market" would respond with righteous indignation. Marc in turn would rant that people had to understand that he made natural wines (this was well before the "natural wine" movement), and if they didn't store his wines correctly, it wasn't his damn fault. Distributors often had hot warehouses; stores usually had lousy storage; and consumers frequently kept wine in warm kitchens. He couldn't control these things, and he wasn't going to compromise his wine for commercial reasons. He did, however, refund all the sales of that '97 Pinot Gris.

He has made a point that only a philistine would ignore. He said that in a year such as 2001, nature gave him grapes lean with minerality; in 2002 she gave him grapes rich with botrytis; and in the torrid year of 2003, she gave him grapes fat with sugar. That's what she dealt, and that's what he worked with. He didn't turn to the powders and potions available in modern cellars to make a consistent product (make no mistake: There's a whole Pandora's box of tricks out there that is all too often abused in commercial winemaking). So if someone did not like his wine from a given vintage for stylistic reasons, that was fine —*so long as they understood what he had to work with and thus respected his effort.*

He has fine-tuned things. But he remains the idealist, marching to the beat of no drummer but his own. Over the years he has had me alternately jump for joy and figuratively rip out my hair in frustration any number of times. But in the final reckoning, if there were ever a wine that made the reach over the rainbow worthwhile, it would be one of his home runs.

One summer evening in 2009 I sat in the Tempé kitchen with Marc, Anne-Marie, my buddy Mark Vlossak from Oregon, and the cellar master of a famous domaine in Alsace. The cellar master was a friend of the Tempés and this was our first meeting. Marc had brown-bagged a bunch of wines for us to taste blind. The cellar master made no real effort to identify the wines beyond identifying them as one of Marc's or not one of Marc's. He liked to speak in metaphorical terms. "This," he said about one wine with extraordinary length that captivated us toward the end of the evening, "makes you think of walking down a long corridor, with light at the end, and it's clear, precise light, without fog, thanks to the limestone this wine comes from. Yet there are doors on all sides of the corridor, open, and full of light also. Precision is what the limestone gives this wine; the many doors, they are open thanks to his hand," he said, indicating Marc. Marc actually lowered his eyes and shook his head against the praise, which made me smile because modesty was not normally a trait I associated with him. As for the wine, it was the 2005 Mambourg Grand Cru Gewurztraminer.

The cellar master was right every time he guessed a wine to be one of Marc's. Early on, it became easy to tell what he would guess by watching him at the first inhalation of a wine's aromas. If he smiled, you knew. The smile led to repeated inhalations, followed by full mouthfuls that he would savor with his eyes shut, and then swallow. "I cannot spit these wines," he told Vlossak and me. "*Le vin est toujours la vie*, which is less and less true, and I cannot spit such a life. They are too rare in our day."

"*Le vin est toujours la vie?*" Vlossak asked.

"Wine is always life," I answered.

"And these lives," the cellar master said, "have such originality."

Chapter 9

LEPRECHAUNS

*I*t was difficult detouring to Besançon the next morning. The exit off the autoroute dropped down into the city, and I begrudged Joe the stop. The newer neighborhoods crept up the hillside, but the old *centreville* lay at the base, and there we went. We just drove around, not having a lot of time because we had an appointment to keep, and with mixed emotions Joe recognized old haunts here and there. He pointed out a couple of academic buildings where he had taken classes, but otherwise he didn't say a lot, he just looked eagerly. To me it appeared to be a provincial city with volumes of history, bustling but without obvious charm, and no doubt it was an interesting place if you had the time to probe its depths. But I didn't have the time, and that was the difficulty. I was forever imagining Andrew Marvell's winged chariots hastening to snatch me to the poetic heavens before the work was completed. I had found a producer in Sancerre, one in Chassagne-Montrachet, and another in Alsace. Three. Three was nothing. I was expected to come home with a portfolio.

I didn't even stop the car to let Joe walk around, which made me feel like a cad. Everything that morning made me feel like a cad: the pressure of time, my insecurity about succeeding, my resentment toward Joe for taking us on this sentimental sideshow, my inability to relax—it was all one big downer. Thirty minutes later, we were back on the autoroute. An hour later, we crossed the Saône River and its plain and then turned south away from Dijon. The trip was almost over. The autoroute took us alongside Beaune, and I found myself wishing instinctively and intensely that we were returning there. The Côte's great flank splayed out in the distance, resplendent even in winter. I knew it now, however slightly, and I was struck by the touch and pull of the familiar in a foreign land.

I wondered how Joe felt returning to Besançon.

We continued south. The comfort of the Côte d'Or disappeared. It was maniacal, I thought, what I was doing, rushing from one farmer to another. The trip was scheduled that way, of course: I had to pack in as much as possible if I wanted to do a halfway decent job. But it was possible to be rushed without being self-absorbed.

I let up on the gas at that point. I tried to settle into a reasonable speed. I don't know if Joe noticed. I figured if I said, Hey, I'm slowing down, he'd look at me like I was a moron. Instead, after a moment, I asked, "So tell me about your year in Besançon."

He frowned. He asked, "What do you mean?"

"Well, I mean, did you like it?"

"Sure," he said. "I did, in fact. I learned a language. I got to be a good skier. It was exciting. It was new. How about you—did you like your year in London?"

"Sure," I said. I shrugged. "I hitchhiked all over the UK. I heard fabulous folk music in Ireland—that was really neat. I watched the Scots celebrate the New Year with massive amounts of whiskey. That was not so neat. The problem was I never had any money. Sometimes I would cheat on the bus just to save a lousy ten pence."

Joe nodded. "I used to pocket lunch food from the cafeteria for dinner later," he said.

"I used to peel off the price tag from a little chicken and put it on a big chicken," I said.

Joe paused. "You did what?"

I rephrased: "I used to cut into the profits of the supermarket."

"You *embezzled* chickens?"

"Hey, a big roast chicken went a long ways!"

"Did you at least roast it with garlic and rosemary," he asked, "or did you throw it in the oven with the plastic still on?"

I looked at him. "Salt and pepper," I said. "I used salt and pepper. I would have had to steal garlic and rosemary."

"Oh, thank God for tender morality!"

"Listen," I said, "don't be a jerk."

"My little brother," he laughed. "A two-bit chicken embezzler!"

"I'm telling you," I insisted, "a big roast chicken went a long ways!"

"Chicken embezzler!"

After a while, we calmed down. We continued driving. We climbed a long hill and descended past these
oversize cartoon characters on the side of the road, courtesy, I supposed, of an imaginative autoroute administra-
tor. They were playing among oversize mushrooms. They
were made of ceramic or plastic and looked like lepre-
chauns. "Look," I said, "the Mushroom People."

Joe looked. He had gone quiet. Maybe going to
Besançon and brushing up against his memories had
taken him there. He watched the Mushroom People pass
by the window. He kept looking out the window and
launched on a riff about when he planted trees for the
Forest Service after college. "I have this vivid memory,"
he said, "of the afternoon when I saw a flock of western
tanagers out on the Montana prairie near the Jefferson
and Madison Rivers, near where they met, south of
Bozeman. My tree-planting buddies and I were recover-
ing from hypothermia when I saw them. We got caught
in a summer snowstorm in the middle of the night trying
to walk the seven miles from Bozeman to Five Corners,
where we knew some people. We were drunk and found
out at three a.m. that all the hotel rooms in Bozeman were
booked because the Montana State University graduation *and* the National Collegiate Rodeo Championships
both took place that weekend. We had picked a bad night
to come in from the woods and celebrate the end of a
planting contract. So we started walking to Five Corners,
and it started raining, and then it started snowing hard. I

was wearing a T-shirt, a light corduroy jacket, and tennis shoes without any socks. When we finally got out to the trailer park where our friends lived around seven a.m., the three of us were in pretty bad shape. They lit a fire in the woodstove and bundled us up in blankets and fed us coffee. We sat and shivered for a few hours, then finally slept. That afternoon the sun came out and it was a sublimely beautiful summer June day, so we all drove out to the river for a picnic. I walked out into the sagebrush and was just standing there astonished at the beauty of the prairie—I think I was in a strange mood due to the mild hypothermia—when a large flock of these little red-gold birds came twittering through, moving fast but stopping from time to time. They were all around me for an instant, then gone. They felt like a little miracle, they were so beautiful. Later I looked them up because I carried a *Peterson's Guide to Western Birds* with me throughout my tree planting. They were western tanagers."

With that, he was done. "I've never seen a tanager," I said.

"I've never seen once since," Joe replied.

"You could have gotten frostbitten feet."

He didn't acknowledge that. Instead, he asked, "Do you think it would be better if he died?"

I drove. Who really wants to play God? Jesus, not me. Then: Who suffers from traumatic brain injury and comes back whole? What comes from the struggle between hope, faith, and reality?

"I don't know," I said.

"Neither do I," Joe replied. "The whole thing just sucks."

It repelled me, what had happened to our father. Here was a man whose own father abandoned him as a child and whose mother could not afford him or his two sisters and so had put them into a children's home in El Paso. He survived that. He survived his youngest son drowning in a farm pond at age three side by side with my cousin of the same age. As a consequence, as I came to understand much later, after one of our many moves, our sisters and Joe and I found ourselves on a swim team in Boston, competing, while Dad learned to sail, as if he were going to take on Poseidon. Or maybe that's wrong. Maybe he just liked sailing because it appealed to his romantic sense of adventure, but he had this horror in the past that he had to deal with, and putting the kids on the swim team accomplished that in some measure.

What I know is that the winter before his accident I followed him up the Shenandoah Valley in the snow. At the farm in the morning six inches already lay on the ground with the snow still falling. Nevertheless, he had a meeting to attend in Pittsburgh, I had to get home in DC, and we both had front-wheel-drive cars. The snow was a problem, he granted, but the real problem was the unplowed and unpaved hill between the interstate and us. So we worked it out that he would take it first and I would follow, each of us gathering speed on the gravel straightaway in hopes that it would propel us over the hill. Two hours later, he signaled an exit, and we got off at Strasbourg to have coffee before going our separate ways.

We had made the hill; we had navigated the all but empty interstate. It had been an exhilarating morning. The snow fell throughout our drive, and the valley pastures were covered with a vivid coat of peaceful whiteness. At the roadside diner, Dad flashed his charismatic smile over his coffee. It was black, his coffee. He always drank it black. "Never," he said, "let the weather stop you, sonny."

Chapter 10

CHEMICAL CHANGES

The Renault had a standard transmission with a gearshift and clutch. The car was faster, and certainly safer, than the five-speed Fiat 124 sports coupe that Dad drove for most of my high school years, but the Renault was nowhere near as fun. The Fiat was nimble, quick, turned on a dime, and was radically different than just about any American car of that era. Every morning we piled into it, and Dad dropped us off at the high school some three miles away before going on to his office. In the afternoons, we walked home. Often I walked with my friend Murphy O'Riley. Murphy went off to some other school in twelfth grade, but not before he cut a deal to buy the Fiat from Dad, who sold it to him for a nominal fee of a hundred bucks.

This allowed the old man to buy a car that emotionally appealed to his driving sensibility, to say nothing of his flamboyant side—an Alfa Romeo hatchback sports coupe. The model, a brand-new one, garnered attention everywhere it went. One memorable afternoon he let me take it to pick up my girlfriend so that we could drive in proper style to our high school graduation. It was a magnificent gesture, and I drove the new car with a great, nervous pride. Except the car never made it. I cut a corner in a park, and another car skidded straight down the hill into us.

No one was hurt, just shook up. The cops and both sets of parents all arrived seemingly simultaneously. The girlfriend's parents looked at me with fierce disapproval (I never did recover my standing) and drove their girl off to her graduation. Dad looked at the situation and directed his not inconsiderable disbelieving anger at one of the cops for refusing to note the length of the skid marks of the other car as evidence of speeding. He was right in the cop's face. He never once yelled at me or chastised me. He took the accident as one of life's lessons in humility and maturity that both of us would be measured by.

At Mâcon Sud I shifted the Renault gently down the ladder of gears, and Joe and I exited the autoroute. We drove toward the ridgeline. The countryside was quaint, full of hills and dales and dotted with pristine villages whose houses sported red clay roof tiles—the first sign of the south. The skyline was dominated by two historic cliffs, that of Solutré and the Roche de Vergisson, one following the other in profile. Prehistoric man stampeded animals off these cliffs for food, and in the soil at the base of Solutré, archaeologists have trenched through a layer of bones over three feet thick (six feet, according to another source).

Joe mentioned the abbey of Cluny. He had been studying the map and pointed out that it lay just to the northwest up a little valley that runs by La Roche-Vineuse. The Rock of Vineuse is another huge outcropping in this skyline, rising near the crossroads of the Mâconnais and the Beaujolais, where Burgundy's limestone meets Beaujolais's granite (those plate shifts are responsible for this region's dense contours). The abbey, Joe said, was founded in 910, and by the middle of the twelfth century, some 460 monks lived there in what was the seat of power of the Benedictine order, an order that had spread throughout Europe. During the heyday of the Benedictines' strength, he went on, the abbot of Cluny wielded power like the Pope.

Clearly, Cluny was a place to visit. And clearly a visit to there wasn't part of the schedule. It wasn't until the end of 2006 that I finally took the leisurely D-981 down through the Côte Chalonnaise to Cluny and spent a few hours there. That road was one of the twelfth-century pilgrimage routes to Santiago del Compostella, or Saint Jacques de Compostelle, the legendary resting place of the apostle Saint James in Spain. This particular route started in Vézelay, wound down through the Chalonnaise to Cluny, and thence on to Spain (who said medieval people weren't intrepid travelers?). Pilgrims sewed scallop shells onto their hats or frocks, after the scallops found on the coast of Brittany where the saint's body was said to have been brought ashore. (Alternatively, his body was said to have washed ashore in Spain, covered in scallops;

alternatively still, legend has it that James rescued a drowning knight and the knight emerged from the sea covered in scallops. Any one of these stories accounts for the fact that scallops in France are known as *coquilles St. Jacques*, or Saint James scallops.) The route passed by vineyards that were later named for James, such as in Gevrey where the Aficionado squatted in the snow one desperate morning, or the exquisite Clos St Jacques vineyard in the appellation of Rully, farmed by Domaine de La Folie.

Instead of Cluny, however, Joe and I were scheduled to visit a cooperative. But I was no longer in a hurry, and the pastoral countryside encouraged this mood. The truth is, being mean-spirited about Joe's visit to Besançon, followed by his question about Dad, had thrown me off my dime. I didn't have it in me right then to continue at full throttle. So I putted along the country road. I told Joe how Hemingway drove up through here in the 1920s with F. Scott Fitzgerald. He wrote about this in *A Moveable Feast*, his bitter memoir about his early life in Paris. I engaged Joe in that long-ago drive because it was a good story, and I felt like talking. Hemingway, I said, was cruel in his depiction of Fitzgerald as a weak man whose cylinders, if you took Hemingway's description at face value, seriously misfired after the intake of alcohol. But then, Hemingway's cylinders ran all too smoothly with drink.

I recounted how the two of them went to pick up Fitzgerald's little Renault in Lyon, where Fitzgerald and his wife, Zelda, had abandoned it to a mechanic for repair and hopped on a train for Paris. The journey immediately started out on the wrong foot, with Fitzgerald failing to appear for the morning train from Paris and Hemingway taking it alone to Lyon. The following morning Fitzgerald showed up at Hemingway's hotel and insisted on eating breakfast there, rather than in a much less expensive and quicker cafe. Then he insisted on the hotel preparing them a lunch for the road, which, Hemingway wrote, "could not have cost us very much more than four or five times what it would have cost us if we had bought it for ourselves." Even so, Hemingway, ever solicitous, further observed:

> Scott had obviously been drinking before I met him and, as he looked as though he needed a drink, I asked him if he did not want one in the bar before we set out. He told me he was not a morning drinker and asked if I was. I told him it depended entirely on how I felt and what I had to do and he said that if I felt that I needed a drink, he would keep me company so I would not have to drink alone. So we had a whisky and Perrier in the bar while we waited for the lunch and both felt much better.

Alas, Hemingway's improved disposition didn't last long. To his astonishment, the Renault turned out to be missing its convertible top. Zelda had had the top removed because it had been damaged. Apparently, she liked her cars permanently open-topped. After pointing out Fitzgerald's failings as a mechanic, Hemingway's narration puts them on the road north, parallel to the Saône.

In that day we were halted by rain possibly ten times.

Nonetheless, they appeared to have enjoyed the region's famed blue-footed Bresse chicken, packed by the hotel for their exorbitant lunch, which they washed down with white Mâcon wine straight from the bottle at stops under trees waiting out the passing rainfall. The going must have been slow. In those days the roads had to have been dirt with perhaps a layer of shingle, and they probably only averaged thirty or forty miles an hour. Today it takes less than an hour to drive from Lyon to the city of Mâcon on the autoroute, whereas back then it probably took closer to three hours. With stops for rain and for lunch, even more.

At Mâcon I bought four more bottles of excellent wine which I uncorked as we needed them.

It's not clear how many of those four additional bottles were consumed that day, but given that our intrepid travelers didn't have raincoats, they probably had more need than not for the wine. What is clear is that by the end of the day the rain came harder and harder, and Fitzgerald became convinced that he would die of what he called congestion of the lungs, a uniquely European malady. At Châlon-sur-Saône they stopped for the night at a hotel, and Fitzgerald immediately went to bed. But rather than sleeping, he demanded a thermometer. Hemingway obliged by finding a waiter and giving him money for a thermometer and aspirin, and he ordered two double whiskies and lemon juice for the room. While waiting for the whisky, he finished one of the bottles of Mâcon that they had opened at the last stop. He wished for something "a little more authoritative in preparation for dinner," but the wine had to do.

At last the whisky came, but not the thermometer. Fitzgerald demanded that Hemingway make clear to the waiter the seriousness of the situation. Fitzgerald had by then gone white as a sheet. According to Hemingway, this is what happened to Fitzgerald when he overindulged in alcohol — a fact that Hemingway was only then apparently becoming aware of. Hemingway spoke to the waiter, and then mixed the whisky sours. While they drank them, the waiter returned with a bath thermometer. Dryly, Hemingway commented that at least it wasn't a rectal thermometer, and he pressed it under Fitzgerald's arm. The result showed no fever, and Fitzgerald realized that his recuperative powers had won the day. His relief was palpable; his color returned. He finished his drink with satisfaction and asked for another one. Hemingway ordered another round from room service. This they drank, then Fitzgerald went downstairs in his robe to place a call to Zelda. When he returned, the waiter brought yet another round of double whiskies (the implication is that Fitzgerald ordered them).

Eventually their clothes arrived from being dried, and they dressed and went downstairs for dinner. They each had a plate of escargots and ordered a carafe of Beaujolais from the village of Fleurie "to start with." In the midst of eating his snails, Fitzgerald's call went through, and he disappeared to talk to Zelda for an extended period of time. In the course of waiting, Hemingway polished off Fitzgerald's snails and the carafe of Beaujolais. Fitzgerald returned and ordered a dinner of chicken because they were still in the land of the blue-footed chicken. With this dish, they ordered a bottle of Montagny, a "light, pleasant white wine of the neighborhood." Fitzgerald sipped at his glass, then promptly passed out at the table. Hemingway and the waiter took him up to bed, and Hemingway came back down to finish his dinner and, we must presume, the bottle of Montagny. Such was their day driving through the region.

"I don't remember any of that," Joe said. "I read that book so long ago. All I remember is that they really did drink like fish in the twenties. But it's funny he made Fitzgerald out to be the tragic figure, considering how depressive Hemingway was. He was an insomniac, you know. That probably helped hook him on the booze. In the end, he was such a mess that he went to see a shrink, and he ended up having electric shock therapy, and that completely fried his short-term memory. It tipped him over the edge, and he blew his brains out.

"John Huston," he continued, "the director, said it was a brave act, because the man saw that he was doomed and there was no way out." Joe let that sink in. "They were tough guys back in that generation."

He was right; that sounded pretty tough. "You think it was true," I asked, "that there was no way out?"

"I don't know. It would sure make the act a lot easier. I suspect that Hemingway spent his whole life trying to figure the whole thing out. His life and life in general, that is. It's why he wrote. But there was no figuring out what it's all about because life is one of life's eternal questions."

I smiled. "Ah, yes, the eternal questions."

"Yeah," he said. "The eternal questions. Like, why'd she do it?"

We both laughed out loud at that one. "So what do you think," I asked, "those two great white hunters, Huston and Hemingway, what kind of wine do you think they drank on their safaris?"

"Zinfandel!" he declared. "They drank Zinfandel. They didn't screw around with prissy French wine."

"Naw," I said. "Not Zinfandel. I bet they drank Chateau Latour after plugging their lions and tigers. At least I bet Huston did."

"Heck, who knows," he said. "Whatever they drank, I bet it was tasty with grilled gazelle steaks. And dollars to donuts, they didn't use garlic and rosemary."

"No?"

"No," he said, shaking his head. "They used spices. It was Africa, a continent with centuries of trading with the Indians. Huston and Hemingway, they probably had a very cool rub to put on their gazelle steaks."

We pulled up before the cooperative. It stood on the out-skirts of an old village in the shadow of the first great row of hills, not far from the autoroute. We understood at once how different this was going to be from a visit to a fam-ily domaine. A nicely paved parking lot awaited us, and a sparkling reception hall gleamed with welcome. We felt shabby in our jeans. Warily, we went into that well-lit building, and it proved to be a walk into the lion's den of modern industrial winemaking. The place was a tank farm, a factory for wine production. It had just about any type of wine we might have wanted from the Mâconnais, and its staff, ever helpful, had all manner of labels to offer—or we could create our own. Anything was possible. I could order my own cuvée, large or small, filtered as I wished so long as it was indeed thoroughly filtered, and slap on my very own label. It was a tantalizing thought, however brief. The wines were as cheap and bland as fast food.

An older, dapper commercial agent walked us to our car that sunlit afternoon (the sun was shining!). He shook our hands vigorously and waved, offering a part-ing *A bientôt!* Off we drove, and Joe pointed out that with such a familiar goodbye a relationship was anticipated—that they had us, so they hoped, in their clutches. I didn't like the idea. It wasn't just the quality. It was also the fact that there was no person behind the wine, no man or woman working their parcel of vines to make what we had in bottle, no connection to a place.

In the village we stopped for a shot of espresso at a bar. Inside, a handful of locals stood before their little glasses of wine with cigarettes between their fingers. Their conversation ceased as we walked in. But their smoke lingered, and after we got our coffee and the bit of chocolate that accompanied it, they resumed their quiet talk with the bartender. I still couldn't understand a damn word they were saying, but they didn't know that and they hadn't completely frozen us out. That gave reason for hope.

"I'm not going to do any business with the co-op," I told Joe.

"Okay," he said. "It's your show."

It was nice of him to back me up. It drove home the fact that we weren't kids anymore.

We drove through the village of Vinzelles and passed its co-op, housed in a big building down at the round-about. From there we climbed up the first ridge off the autoroute, following signs for Fuissé. Pouilly-Fuissé is the premier appellation in the Mâconnais and takes its name from its two reigning villages. This was another appellation that I knew well from bottles and books, and as we came up the hill from Vinzelles, I was all eyes before the hallowed land. The little road coursed up through one vineyard after another until we crested the ridge and, lo and behold, looked upon Fuissé. The village sat snug in the depths of a deep bowl, surrounded on three sides by immense hills, each regal flank stitched with vines. A great church rose above the village, giving it a solemn air.

We stopped the car and scrambled up on a bank for a better view.

"Fuissé!" I exclaimed. *Fuee-ʃay.* It had a ring to it.

"Man," Joe said, "this is beautiful. Can you imagine if we rented a place in these hills and everyone came out for vacation? There's wine, food, culture, history, hiking — everything. It's perfect."

"You speak the language."

"You know the wine."

"We have the resources!"

We jumped back in the car and went down the switchback road for a look around. After determining the whereabouts of our next morning's appointment, we drove up out of the bowl and dipped into another dale and into the appellation of Beaujolais for an appointment with the de Boissieu family at their huge house named Lavernette. God knows how old that great manor is. In 1596 the Lavernette family bought it from the monks of the Abbey of Tournus, and thereafter the family's descendants ate the doves that populated the elegant stone dovecote in an adjacent pasture, made wine from the property's vineyards, and helped Napoléon fight his wars. Then, in the early part of the twentieth century, Bertrand de Boissieu's grandfather married the heiress of the Château de Lavernette, and the château changed hands.

The de Boissieus were an important French family, as might be gleaned from the prefix *de* (it indicates nobility). An early notable was Jean-Jacques de Boissieu, an eighteenth-century finance counselor to the king. More importantly, he was an engraver whose works can be seen in the Louvre, the Met, and any number of other museums around the world. Then the page of history turns to Bertrand's first cousin once removed, one Alain de Boissieu. He was Charles de Gaulle's son-in-law and a famous general in his own right (in one of history's last cavalry charges, he pulled out his saber and successfully led his troops against a German force during the 1940 invasion of France). At the height of the political crisis gripping Paris in May 1968, President de Gaulle secretly flew to the headquarters of the French army in Germany to meet the French commander—a meeting arranged by General de Boissieu. De Gaulle did this to secure the backing of the French army, something none too secure at the time. The commander agreed to support the president on the condition that he free one of the generals who had led a failed *coup d'état* in 1961 during the terribly controversial negotiations leading up to Algeria's independence. That general had gotten as far as emplaning paratroopers in Algiers to fly to France before the coup collapsed and he was tossed in jail. De Gaulle accepted the condition and returned to Paris to dissolve the National Assembly.

If such colorful history informed Bertrand de Boissieu, Joe and I could not tell even had we known about it. He met us that afternoon in the Lavernette courtyard, a quiet and seemingly laid-back country squire who pruned his own vines and favored jeans. Later I would learn that in his formative years Bertrand hitchhiked around Europe and Africa instead of pursuing a career in the military, and married an engaging Dutch girl named Anke. She was, I would discover, a talented cook. But the history of his uncle, this I learned by happenstance years later when I read a book on the liberation of Paris and the political aftermath, an aftermath that continues to play itself out today.

Anke joined us in the courtyard, a vast affair of dirt and gravel with a towering chestnut tree in front of the sandstone-colored manor house, which had rows of windows framed by big white shutters. After touring the modest winery in back, they took us into the original kitchen in a wing off the main house. We sat around a table in front of an old, open-face brick oven and tasted. The wines were a sparkling crémant, a Beaujolais Blanc, two Pouilly-Fuissés, and two Beaujolais-Villages. Each reflected the best of the region, being above all easy and soothing and a real pleasure to drink. They did this deftly, much as Bertrand carried off his relaxed demeanor. That's what you first saw, that's what you first experienced, but if that was all there was, then things wouldn't be that interesting. Underneath his calm facade, Bertrand was a serious and hardworking man. Under a mouthful of enticing appley fruit, a good Mâcon (or, in this case, a rarer Beaujolais Blanc) is made toothsome in the hands of better *vignerons* by its cut and stony finish. Similarly, a good red Beaujolais is delicious by virtue of the simplicity of its exuberant red pit fruit. When simplicity does the trick, that's a neat thing. These are wines you can return to again and again without tiring; they're not ponderous. Hemingway understood this very well, and he took a thoroughly enlightened approach to wine:

> In Europe then we thought of wine as something as healthy and normal as food and also as a great giver of happiness and well being and delight. Drinking wine was not a snobbism nor a sign of sophistication nor a cult; it was as natural as eating and to me as necessary, and I would not have thought of eating a meal without drinking either wine or cider or beer. I loved all wines except sweet or sweetish wines and wines that were too heavy, and it had never occurred to me that sharing a few bottles of fairly light, dry, white Mâcon could cause chemical changes in Scott that would turn him into a fool.

Fitzgerald, poor fool that he was, never took the time to pen his own account of their wayward journey.

Chapter 11

BEAUJOLAIS

That night we stayed in a forgotten hotel along the old road fronting the first range of hills. The building was down on its luck and all but empty. It was big, with three floors and God knows how many rooms, and probably looked a whole lot better back around the time that Hemingway and Fitzgerald passed through. Our room was cramped, painted a dismal facsimile of sky blue, and offered threadbare towels and worn mattresses. The vast dining room seated only a couple of other travelers that evening, adding to the forlorn ambience. Nonetheless, with pizzazz we ordered *coq au vin*, the only chicken on the menu in the land of chicken. It arrived as dry and tough as beef jerky, covered with a sauce of red wine reduced to little more than a paste. It was so bad that we had to laugh about it.

Breakfast the following morning, however, was better: the coffee strong, the croissants fresh. We had managed to sleep fairly well too, at last, and that made all the difference. Joe pulled up the car as I paid the bill. The proprietor, a gregarious gray-haired man who didn't seem to mind that

I couldn't understand him, held me in conversation as we walked to the courtyard on what was a clear and fabulously refreshing morning. Joe stepped out of the car, and the two of them began an animated discussion concerning the pros and cons of Renaults. The old man stepped over and gave the hood of the car a firm pat of approval. They discussed the state of travel in France today, with Joe complaining about the high tolls on the autoroute and the older man agreeing that this was indeed a grave scandal. Meanwhile, I took in the pebbled carriageway, sweeping through a rambling yard peppered with towering trees and unkempt grass. Long ago, it was clear, our woebegone hotel once had aspirations of grandeur.

We took to the hill for our morning appointment. As we drove up the winding road to Fuissé, I buzzed with energy. A solid night's sleep, I thought, was a gift from the gods.

"Well," I said, "are you ready for the morning's first, bracing shot of Chardonnay?"

"I can't wait!" Joe replied, evidently feeling rather energized himself.

"I know what you mean," I said. "It's a fine road, this road to dissolution."

"It *is* a fine road," he agreed. "And the amazing thing is, it meets the requirements of the job!"

We paused on the crest of the hill to look upon the garden bowl of Fuissé, and then coasted down the switchback road. In the village the proprietor of the domaine we came to visit welcomed us in. He was well-groomed, dressed in a polo shirt, and he struck me right away as a thirty-something American who had grown up in a wealthy suburb. He was definitely not one of the men-of-the-soil types. This soured me; I wanted to like this property. It had a smart label and the wine had the pedigree of Pouilly-Fuissé—there was obvious commercial possibility. I knew my reaction to the man was a knee-jerk one, and I tried to keep an open mind. We went into the cellar to taste the wines (he had Mâcon-Villages and Pouilly-Vinzelles, as well as Pouilly-Fuissé). They were solid, marketable, and all too similar. And expensive. His car outside was expensive too.

For the sake of argument, I pushed him a little on the price, but that went nowhere. Had I been confident enough about the wines to make a serious offer, we could have had a real conversation, but what kept intruding upon my thinking was that these were not passionate wines in the mode of Marc Tempé. Nor were they delicious wines that reflected their place with real style like those of the de Boissieus at Lavernette. Instead, these were commercial wines designed to please the greatest common denominator in the marketplace. They were like the co-op's wines, better and pricier, but made with the same ethic. I had to make a choice about how I wanted to proceed.

Back in our Renault, I took a moment before turning the key. "I'm glad we found Bertrand de Boissieu," I said.

"He is a more dependable man," Joe observed.

"He's got his feet on the ground," I said.

"His wines have more *typicité*."

"And more character."

"Speaking of such things, Royboy," Joe said, opening the atlas, "we have a choice. We can get on the autoroute now, or we can take these little D roads and explore the crus of the haut Beaujolais, and then get on the autoroute farther south. What say you?"

I didn't say anything right away. I looked at the map. "I make this right turn at the top of the hill instead of going straight for the autoroute, don't I?"

"You do. Are we on?"

"Why not?"

"Hey," Joe smiled, "Beaujolais, here we come!"

We wound our way through Chaintré and by Château de Lavernette, and in Juliénas we stopped to buy things for lunch, much as we had on the road to Burgundy. I got the bread, Joe got the pâté, and we found a store from which to buy water, cheese, and apples. Somewhere south of Fleurie we stopped on a small plateau, but in contrast to that first lunch when the cold damp kept us in the car, now the sun shone brightly. We got out and walked to the middle of a vineyard, where a farmer long ago had established a little dumping ground for rocks, brush, the odd piece of machinery, and even an old wood pallet.

Joe pulled out a rock to sit on, put the baguette on the pallet, and opened a penknife to start slicing. On a whim, I did something that I would never have done earlier in the trip. Maybe Hemingway inspired me, or maybe I just wanted to lighten up. In any event, I went back to the car and returned with a bottle of Lavernette's Beaujolais — it would have been sacrilegious to drink anything but Beaujolais here — and put it down on the pallet. "Well," Joe commented happily, "truly, we *are* on the road to dissolution!" I laughed and said that some wine seemed reasonable. "Yes," he said, "and we are ever reasonable!"

We sat there in our oasis and ate in a luxurious mood, looking over the sandy vineyard to the valleys and hills before us, taking the bottle off the pallet now and again to drink straight from it just as Fitzgerald and Hemingway had with their bottle(s) of Mâcon. Like them, we didn't have any glasses. This added to the ambience, and we found ourselves laughing. At one point, I looked over the landscape and thought about how we were exploring classical winemaking and its traditions, traditions that were tied to seasons and perforce were slow and rhythmical. Such things stood in stark contrast to my characteristic impatience. Dad had been fond of saying that impatience was the most underrated of virtues. Joe, on the other hand, studied maps to find the leisurely byroads. We grew up thinking we each knew best and that our ways were the only ways to do things, but I realized I couldn't very well assert that now. Given that I didn't much feel like asserting it, this settled in as a nice thought.

As it is wont to do, however, time pushed us along. Joe picked up the cork to put into the bottle. Then he paused. He pointed to the wine and asked me, "You're not going to pull a Fitzgerald and turn chemical on me now, are you?"

Chapter 12

SUBLIME PROSPECTS

ertrand de Boissieu had told us that driving straight through the center of Lyon was the most direct route south, if we hit the city in midday rather than during the morning or evening rush hour (the alternative was to take the long ring road around). Talk about a ride! The autoroute bore right into the city, climbing on its approach, then plunging down a harrowing hill to scoot over a chasm, then tunneling under a hill, bridging the Saône, tunneling again and immediately, upon exiting into daylight, whipping into a ninety-degree turn to parallel the Rhône River. All this was done in a manner that would make an American civil engineer shudder at the possibility of accidents and lawsuits. But no matter: Onward we drove and throughout we navigated successfully, drinking in as much of the city as we could along the way. It was big and industrial, full of historic buildings, majestic buildings, and ugly buildings, and it had an old quarter that we gleefully caught snatches of as we rode the wave of traffic rolling southward.

Then the city fell behind us. We followed the now mighty Rhône River through its industrial outskirts. We crossed a bridge that funneled the traffic onto the river's east bank, and southward we drove on what was now named the Autoroute du Soleil. We were hemmed in on all sides by trappings of urbanization sprawling up the hillsides and spilling out of this narrow valley. Soon enough, however, we climbed a final rise to crest a plateau and found ourselves back in the country-side. In rapid succession, we passed the appellations of Condrieu and Côte-Rôtie and headed for the appellation of Hermitage (the former the cradle of Viognier, the latter two the cradle of Syrah). Though we did not know it at the time, we were following in famous footsteps. In March of 1787 Thomas Jefferson traveled along the Rhône in his own carriage drawn by three horses. Of this stretch of country between Côte-Rôtie and Hermitage, he wrote:

> Nature never formed a country of more savage aspect than that on both sides of the Rhône. A huge torrent, rushing like an arrow between high precipices often of massive rock, at other times of loose stone with but little earth. Yet has the hand of man subdued this savage scene, by planting corn where there is little fertility, trees where there is still less, and vines where there is none. On the whole, it assumes a romantic, picturesque, and pleasing air.

All of this would have been much more obvious had we not been flying down the highway at eighty miles per hour. Soon enough, however, we exited the autoroute at Tain l'Hermitage. I told Joe how the Rhône made an abrupt jog, or so I'd read, uniquely exposing the southern flank of a huge hill that came to be named Hermitage for reasons lost to history. There is a story about a wounded knight who returned from a crusade disheartened by his fellow man. In the early thirteenth century, he supposedly retreated to this hill and on top, closest to God, built himself a chapel. There he lived ever after. But this is too romantic for some to stomach and so it is disputed, and lost to time as well is who first cultivated vines on this flank (the Romans, or the Greeks before them?). Later in the day Jefferson made a visit, and he must have thought that subduing this proud, steep hillside with terraces and vines was worth the extraordinary effort, for in his diary he noted that white Hermitage was "the first wine in the world without a single exception." He liked the sweeping declarative. He liked the hill's red wine too, remarking on its solid constitution and even more so on its perfume, which, he noted, is often compared to that of raspberries—as it is today.

What motivated us, however, was not history nor wine but rather the chance to get some exercise. We wanted to hike up that hill. We had been doing little more than sitting in a car or at a table eating and drinking for over a week. It must be factored in that the food was different too, with more fat than we were used to (pâtés, rillettes, and duck confit, along with, of course, the endless array of cheeses), and only half jokingly we argued over whether chicken was the vegetable in a given meal. Our constitutions were altogether plugged. We had both run cross-country and track in high school, and Joe had raced road bikes. We didn't like feeling like a couple of lard buckets.

The town of Tain had something of a picturesque quality, but not much in the way of a pleasing air. In fact, it was pretty dank and dismal. The hand of man, unlike that of nature, hasn't been terribly successful aesthetically with the towns and villages in the northern Rhône Valley. To the south the valley opens, the sun pours in, and the languid atmosphere of Provence envelops; up north, the ambience is somehow more restricted, like the geography. Up north too, industry developed.

But the hill of Hermitage . . . there it was, a high precipice to be sure, covered with a great vest of vines stitched across what could be seen as a broad chest of earth rising steeply behind the waterfront town. The best place to take it all in proved to be the midway point of the footbridge that traversed the Rhône. "Who would have thought," Joe said, "that there'd be a pedestrian bridge linking two little towns facing each other across this river. What a good idea." The bridge crossed the center of the bend the river took around the hill, and the river itself was all twirls and mean-looking below, ruled by a fearsome current. But up above on the bridge, facing the town, the scene was tranquil.

From that point we picked out where we would ascend, then walked through the narrow town and found a stony path. The way up veered toward a ravine that formed a fold in the hillside, and we went by one terrace after another, each with its two or three or four rows of vines. This was not productive ground, nor was it pro- lific in terms of acreage. It was easy to imagine a grower working his half a dozen terraces, hoeing the ground by hand (or spraying weed killer), nursing baby vines with inordinate care because every one counted, rebuilding the stone walls when time and energy permitted and when necessity required, harvesting by hand and carrying the grapes down the hill on his back, and then either selling his crop to the co-op or his wine to *négociants* or, maybe, bottling it himself to sell out of his door. It was a living. A small grower like that wouldn't earn much money, but he owned his land outright and wasn't beholden to a bank.

We passed growers as we climbed. There weren't many, and with a glance each one determined that we were outsiders and so turned their eyes back to what lay at hand on their terrace. One was ungainly tall and dark- haired, pruning vines, and I remember him because sev- eral years later I visited someone very much like him in Tain. This man was skinny as a rail and towered over me like Abe Lincoln. He was cursed with bad teeth, and quite a few had been crowned with silver-colored white gold, so as he spoke I found myself looking up into a silver mine. He made a pure, aromatic style of Hermitage and Croze- Hermitage, and he railed against the current fashion for what he called monster (*mun-stra!*) wines. I mentioned a young grower in one of the Côtes-du-Rhône villages who was gaining fame for cutting his yields from a normal thirty-five hecoliters per hectare to about seventeen. This made for a very concentrated wine at the expense of finesse. To my surprise, the concentration also dumbed down the aromatics. *"Un vin comme ça, c'est un monstre, un monstre!"* Abe spit, clearly sharing Hemingway's dislike of heavy wines. One needs a *balanced* yield, he went on, not a huge or tiny yield, to express the *terroir*. At this, he articulated the view that the strength of French viticulture lies in its historic evolution, whereby specific varieties came to be planted in places that lay at the limit of their ripening. Thus, Pinot Noir and Chardonnay in Burgundy; Chenin Blanc in the Loire; Grenache in the southern Rhône; and of course Syrah in the northern Rhône. Any farther north, and these grapes would not normally ripen. This growing on the cusp of ripeness provides a high-toned aromatic nuance and a vibrant depth and complexity of flavor that otherwise would not be possible. (Global warming may be screwing up this evolutionary balance, but that's a story for another book.)

On we climbed, going as fast as we could without breaking our stride. We humped by more than thirty terraces, going all but straight up in that fold in the hill. At the last bit we scrambled, running, racing until we suddenly mounted a peak. We stood there catching our breath. The crusader's chapel, or rather a modern rendition, sat on an adjacent peak. We turned to look at Tain and down a length of the Rhône River. From this vantage point the surface of the river was placid and gave no sign of the pulsating current underneath. The air was serene on our peak, save for our breathing. Jefferson, a fan of exercise himself, had made the climb too:

> Go up to the top of the hill, for the sake of the sublime prospect from thence.

In Jefferson's day there may not have been a foot-bridge, and certainly there would not have been the auto-route; the town would have been smaller, the population less dense. Otherwise, what we looked at was in essence what he looked at in 1787. Probably there was more cultivation on the steep hillsides framing the Rhône, but the shape of those hillsides and their peaks, the plains on the other side, and the river itself had not changed.

After a while, Joe said, "I think we need to make this climb a couple more times to make a dent in all the lard we've gained."

I agreed wholeheartedly. But the world conspired against us. We had an appointment; we had to get to Châteauneuf-du-Pape.

Chapter 13

PROVENCE

o we got back onto the Highway of the Sun and continued south. The road climbed one particularly steep
hill that hemmed in the river, and we pulled off at a vista
stop to look down upon a gray nuclear power plant and a
raw stone quarry cut into the far bank, a bank otherwise
wildly verdant. Soon afterward, the valley opened and
the muscular green hills on either side gave way to craggy
outcroppings and rocky plains. North of Orange we came
off a big plateau, and there in the far distance were more
enormous cooling towers for another nuclear plant. The
sight got us talking about how Dad had taken a bunch of
trips to France in the early and mid-1970s for Westinghouse when it had dealings with Framatone, the French
nuclear agency. From one of those trips he returned and
decided that we would have bread with every dinner, as
the French did, and so in Pittsburgh Mom began to buy
loaves of what the local supermarket labeled Italian bread.

We came upon vineyards just south of the town of
Orange. There we got off the autoroute and drove into

the appellation of Châteauneuf-du-Pape. The road curved and climbed gently among patches of vineyards, one after another after another, broken by ditches or dirt roads marking invisible boundaries, or a slice of gnarly forest here and there where grapes could not profitably grow. It was very dry land, marked by sandy limestone outcroppings and a remarkable profusion of smooth, softball-size stones strewn over the vineyards like chain mail. These were the *galets roulés*, left by glaciers an ice age ago. We stopped to have a closer look. "Wow," Joe said, hefting a *galet* in his hand, "they *plow* this ground?"

"Maybe a farm implement dealership is the business to be in here," I laughed. "You could sell a lot of replacement plows and hitches."

"You're not just whistling Dixie!" Joe agreed. "This stuff must be murder on machinery. It must be murder on man. It must just be murder, period. Why do they bother?"

We stood there a few minutes longer, letting the sense of this place settle in. In Bordeaux, along the Médoc Peninsula, the famous first-growth vineyards grow on the high ground—a relative term, because that peninsula is for all intents and purposes flat and low. But it gently dips and rises, and the rises mark the points of highest deposits left by ice and water back through the ages, and those first-growth vineyards grow on what are effectively gravel mounds. Vines love well-drained soils, and nothing drains better than gravel.

"You know what must happen here?" I said. "When they plow, the dirt gets turned up over these rocks, but then at the first good rain it washes back down under the rocks. That's why it looks like these vines stick up out of a carpet of rocks."

The repository of knowledge didn't dispute this, so I figured I had a pretty good chance of being right. We got back into the car. The road climbed onto a small plateau. In the early fourteenth century, Pope Clement V moved his court from Rome to France, eventually settling in Avignon, some dozen miles farther south along the Rhône from where we were now. At the time, Avignon was held by the king of Sicily, and the land around it was held by the Church. The pope installed himself in Avignon and built a huge fortress of a home for himself and his court, and installed the Curia nearby. His successor bought Avignon from the king of Sicily to add to the surrounding papal land that lay within the kingdom of France. But Avignon sweltered in summer, and the crowds made it worse (largely by overwhelming the town's nonexistent plumbing), thus the successor scouted about until he found this small plateau north of the city. There he could have healthier air and take refuge from the madding crowd in the hot summer months. And so he built himself a second castle, this one linked with other outlying fortifications to protect Avignon, and by the twentieth century this residence had become officially known as the new castle of the pope, or Châteauneuf-du-Pape (its wine, however, had previously been known as *vin de pape*). A village may have already existed before the castle. Who knows? What's certain is that this village became clustered in the lee of the castle, huddling on the plateau's hillside like a footing for the papal bulwark.

To this village we drove. Rounding a final bend, we were greeted by a wall of the castle, impressively tall, one of two walls that remained. It stood straight, crowned by a rampart, a great shield protecting the village. The German army maintained a munitions dump within the castle walls, and during the retreat of 1944 the army blew up the dump. No doubt this did its share of damage, but prewar photographs on the walls of the restaurant La Mère Germaine in the center of the village clearly show that the castle had fallen into ruin long before the war. Possibly two of the four walls crumbled over time, aided by modern explosives. Just as likely, the castle became an impromptu quarry for local builders, unable to resist all that finely cut stone. In any event, the original construction was solid, for those two remaining walls have withstood the mistral wind for decades.

Opposite the post office we found our destination, the Domaine des Sénéchaux. This venerable domaine was purchased in 1993 by Pascal Roux, then the proprietor of Château du Trignon in nearby Gigondas. I didn't know anything about Roux, except that he, like his father before him, sold Trignon's wines to the importer Kermit Lynch. For whatever reason, Lynch chose not to represent Sénéchaux. Importer Bobby Kacher got wind of this and, at the same time that he invited me to meet him in Sancerre, suggested I go see the domaine. A generation before me, Lynch was one of the great champions of artisan French wine, a fact both inspiring and intimidating. Regardless, the appointment was made, and Joe and I found ourselves in the narrow courtyard of the domaine, knocking on the door.

The man who answered was tall and bespectacled. The lower half of his face was wrapped in a bristling brown dragoon's moustache like the Aficionado's (though not so carefully brushed). He welcomed us with a gravelly *accent du soleil* (in Provence Roux is not pronounced *rou*, as up north, but rather *rewks*, with a hard *k*). He stood with his shorter winemaker, a dark-haired, silent fellow from Bandol who, being clean-shaven, looked somehow naked. Sénéchaux, I would learn, had its chef and crew, and Trignon its chef and crew. The two domaines shared only the same owner and his commercial agent.

Pascal invited us in with a shy flourish of his hand. He led the way up a staircase, past walls freshly painted with bright Provençal yellow and red, to the upper level where the light was much darker. Here, from the rear at a higher street level, the domaine received its grapes. On this level the grapes were crushed in a press and dumped into the large concrete fermentation and aging vats underfoot. Each vat had a manhole cover that opened to show a depth of some ten feet to the bottom of the vat. Pascal pointed to one and said, "When we came in 1993, there were no doors cut into the side of the vats along the lower level. They built these vats sometime around the first war—probably just before," he mused, "because there would not have been anyone to build them afterward—and every year since the workers descended into each vat by ladder to clean them with a rope around their chest." He paused, and squinted through his glasses at us. They needed polishing, his glasses. "Think about that: A man had about ten minutes before he was overcome by the gas!" He raised his arms. *"C'était incroyable. Incroyable!"*

He was talking about carbon dioxide, a by-product of fermentation that lingers in tanks where it displaces oxygen. This is a real hazard, and cellar workers around the world suffocate with some regularity. Pascal couldn't fathom the culture that supported such disregard of basic safety. To me, the whole idea was something out of the early days of industrialization. It seemed distant, arcane, foreign—a tale from Charles Dickens. To think that a mere five years ago guys went into these vats with ropes so that they could be pulled out if they were overcome would have been inconceivable to me five minutes before.

"I guess," Joe remarked, "the workers didn't have a very strong union."

Pascal scrutinized him with a squint and laughed loudly behind that broom of a moustache. "No," he said, "I think not!"

With that, he took us back downstairs. It was the sides of the vats that were so brightly painted, I now realized, and there at the base of each one was a gleaming new stainless steel door hatch. Pascal pointed out several big new oak *foudres* as well as 600-liter *demi-muid* barrels and the more normal 225-liter barrels. Most of the wine was aged in the concrete vats, but the various wood vessels were being experimented with and what went into bottle was a combination of all. And all a year's wine, he carefully underscored, was bottled at one time, rather than in several bottlings over time, which was (and is) common practice in the south, making consistency within a given vintage problematic.

Pascal went on to show us the new bottling line. Then he explained how they had to plant new white varieties in the vineyards, as well as new parcels of Syrah and Mourvèdre (*"Hit iz four the nexxt'd generationn,"* he noted in English with a shrug, his broad accent panning out across a riverbed of vocal cords). Fortunately, they were able to salvage the big block of Grenache, planted in the 1930s.

"And tat iz how we doo things at the Sénéchaux," he said.

We nodded. The naked winemaker looked about impatiently. Pascal cleared his throat and adjusted his glasses. "Well," he asked, "would you like to taste now?"

"Avec plaisir," I answered, with unaccustomed boldness. This was, after all, what Joe always said by way of a positive response. I was certain that right then he glanced at me with astonishment, but I would never have been able to keep a straight face had I returned his look.

"D'accord," Pascal replied, and led the way to the tasting room.

I ended up working with Pascal. It was all but a foregone conclusion that I would want to, given his track record at

Trignon, the investment he put into Sénéchaux, and the popularity of Châteauneuf-du-Pape. What we tasted out of the bottle was the 1996 and it was light; what we tasted from vat and barrel was the '97, and it was better but not as good as the 1995, which was sold out. Sénéchaux was a work in progress but a clear winner. Fairly soon in our relationship Pascal parted ways with the winemaker from Bandol, who liked the influence of new wood more than Pascal did, and in came Bernard. He came with an accent to equal Pascal's, plus a bald pate, a chiseled Roman nose, a tall, broad, muscular frame, and a constitution as steady and reliable as the early 1950s-era Perkins tracked tractor that the domaine used to plow through the *galets roulés* every spring. (The secret to plowing those murderous rocks was a tank!) Bernard hit his stride with the 2001 vintage, making a luscious wine brimming with red fruit and kirsch-like ripeness infused with spice and power. Great Grenache is defined by that kind of broad ripeness, and Châteauneuf, Grenache's great home, is defined by power. No other southern French appellation can rival that breadth of power in its wine, which is why Châteauneuf is the undisputed king of those appellations.

Pascal sold Sénéchaux to Jean-Michel Cazes of Bordeaux in 2007. Amid the vast changes in price and distribution that ensued, Cazes did have the wisdom to keep Bernard and his team in place.

The wind had started up during our tasting. We heard its low, steady howl at the door, and once we stepped outside we felt it, but it was not as bad as Marc Tempé's north wind. I was disappointed. This was the famous *mistral* that I had read so much about, a vicious wind that swoops off the cold Alps to whip down the Rhône Valley, sucked south across the Mediterranean by the dry heat of Africa's Sahara Desert. Alsace's north wind, I thought, had it beat.

"*Ah, le mistral,*" Pascal noted, looking upward, the sage native. "*Il commence.*" He laughed. "You must hurry!"

"You mean," I asked, "it gets worse?"

"Oh, yes," he said, suddenly quite serious, his eyes magnifying behind his blurry lenses. His hand made a flourish in the air above his head. "This, this is nothing!"

We hurried. We had some time before the dinner hour. We quickly walked to the center of the little village, past the horrid public restrooms the village had thoughtfully installed for the throngs of tourists (how better to convey an accurate sense of fourteenth-century Avignon?). Fortunately the tourists at this hour, let alone this time of year, were nowhere to be seen. The village center lay somnolently at a sharp turn in the narrow main road, defined by an old plane tree, an old bench or two, and a big, dry fountain. A couple of old guys hung out on the bench, not yet chased inside by the nascent wind. The occasional car whizzed by, and the occasional truck roared by, leaving a spew of diesel fumes in its wake. Talking among themselves, the old guys sat, oblivious to it all.

Directly up from this center went a pedestrian roadway to the remains of the castle. Shops and domaine outlets lined this roadway to sell their wine. We made our way up to the castle to peer within the remaining two

walls, golden with that Provençal hue, age-old with windowless portals placed precisely by an architect's eye.
Inside, the great ground floor lay intact, but the others
above it were long gone, so the two sides of the rectangle
were now only a shell of their former selves and carried
only their own weight. Nonetheless this vertical structure
stood with stately elegance above the village. Ruin, as is
sometimes said, became it. The head wall rose as tall as
the floor was long, which made it tall indeed. On the far
side of the castle, on the plateau itself, a small parking lot
covered the hand of nature, but then beyond the asphalt
came a mass of vineyard spreading north and sloping gently downward. Naturally, the fortification took the high
ground. Far to the east, the white stone-topped mountain
of Ventoux dominated the Alps. It must have been something, this papal summer retreat, back in its prime.

We checked into our hotel west of the village. Night
was falling, and the time had come to make the day's
momentous decision: where to have dinner. This took on
additional weight because our time was nearly up. We only
had one more day in France. The village of Châteauneuf-
du-Pape, however, struck us both as cold and uninviting.

I sat on my bed. Joe sat on his.

"Where to?" I asked.

"Gigondas," he said without hesitation. He scratched
at his beard and looked over to gauge my reaction.

"Gigondas?"

"I mapped it out already," he said. "It's only about a
half hour away."

"Think it has a restaurant?"

He shrugged. He had purpose; I could see this. "Come on," he said.

"Okay," I said. It made sense; we had our final appointment the next day in Gigondas, so a little reconnoitering couldn't hurt. Then a lightbulb went on in my brain—we had drunk Gigondas during Joe's rehearsal dinner. This was in the previous decade. Joe had been married in an historic village in England, and the rehearsal dinner took place in a picture-perfect little timber-and-beam inn built in the fourteenth century. The marriage didn't last, but no one foresaw that then, and we ate lamb and drank Gigondas with abandon. Dad had waxed rhapsodic about the wine, and we were right there with him because it was so authentic, so unique, and so stunningly good with the lamb.

Never, I thought, argue with sentimentality. Besides, I remembered that dinner fondly.

I picked up the keys. We went outside. The wind all but blew us off our feet. "Holy shit!" Joe screamed. The wind stole his words like a purse-snatcher and fled into the night. Pascal hadn't been kidding. I started laughing, but I don't think Joe heard. He was ahead, bent over against this howling current, and when he reached the car, he turned with amazed eyes, which made me laugh harder. I staggered to the car. When I got there, I put my hands on the hood to brace myself, and looked bright-eyed across at Joe. "*Open the fucking car!*" he screamed.

I opened the fucking car. Joe jumped in. I jumped in. "My God!" he exclaimed. "That's not some little blast—that's an unrelenting, unremitting freaking furnace of a wind! That is the *blitzkrieg* of wind!!"

I drove like a beetle in the face of the blitzkrieg. That is, slowly, determinedly, and rather brainlessly, with both hands on the wheel. What business did we have going out in a full-blown windstorm? But it wasn't so bad, at least on the open straightaways, because as Joe said, the wind was constant. It didn't come in bursts and gusts, so you quickly took its measure on a straight road. It was the buildings along the road and turns that alternated the force and made for over- or under-compensation with the steering. At one point, following a serious under-compensation that left me white-knuckled on the steering wheel, Joe hissed: *"Don't kill us!"*

"I won't!" I replied.

We drove on in silence. Then Joe asked: "Does this thing have air bags?"

Air bags were just then becoming standard. I had no idea if the Renault had them, and I didn't want to take my eyes off the road or turn on the inside light to look. Joe, in fact, had just turned off that blasted light after re-checking the map for the third or fourth time. "Of course it does," I said. "The drop-down, self-inflatable kind with a blow tube."

"Ah," he said, "the most dependable kind. Take the right up ahead."

The right turn began our trek up the hill to the old fortified village of Gigondas. We had crossed the autoroute and driven a half a dozen miles or so over a rocky plain that was, so far as we could tell in the night, parceled up and cultivated to its last inch. Boundaries were often marked by windbreaks of vertical cedars whose tops bent gently over in the wind like plumes of ostrich feathers. Except there was nothing gentle about it—the wind shrieked across the plain and forced those tough cedars over. It just looked gently composed because entire rows were bent over, as if in bow.

We drove up to the old village, turned to enter along a narrow road, and came into the little main square. A handful of big old plane trees stood leafless in that barren space. There was a low stone wall before us and the village's few stately buildings behind us. There were only a couple cars present. I turned the engine off, and we sat a moment, listening to the mistral howl. It was pretty dark around us.

"Whew," Joe said. "I'm hungry after all that."

Me too. In fact, I was starving. "That better be a restaurant behind us and not a hotel," I said, referring to the one building that had lights on outside its door and behind its white-curtained windows. We braced ourselves and climbed out into that wind. The doors to the building were a pair of those tall, narrow, *belle-epoch* kind with a thick glass pane inlaid in each door's upper two-thirds. They were elegant doors, and they signaled possibility and hope in a dark and dangerous world.

It *was* a restaurant, thank God. (It still is, although today the owners and the lights are different.) It was small, intimate, and inviting, with white tablecloths. There were only two or three tables taken. The *madame* sat us down. She joked about *le mistral* scaring her customers away. She brought us *apértifs* of the local *vin blanc*. She gave us menus. It was . . . perfect.

Then, diabolically, the thought came to mind that maybe it was *too* perfect. Maybe something would happen. I lowered my menu. "All we have to do now," I said in a near whisper, "is make it back to the hotel alive."

Joe took a mouthful of wine and nearly spewed it across the table in a spasm of laughter. When he had regained enough control to talk, he said, "Maybe, before we take off, we ought to blow up our air bags and tape them to the ceiling of the car, just to be ready."

This brought to mind an image of a couple of guys squeezed into a car with their heads bent over trying to see around two huge beach balls of air bags to drive. I looked at Joe. He was trembling, red-faced, trying to suppress convulsions of laughter that were all too contagious. "Do you think they have any duct tape here?" he gasped.

We soon recovered. In earnest we began to read the menu, which required bringing the candle between us because it was so dark in the restaurant. *Madame* came along and told us the special was a local game bird, freshly shot. Our eyes lit up: This was something you didn't see every day in the States. We both ordered the bird, plus starters and, naturally, a bottle of Gigondas. *Madame* returned with the bottle and pulled the cork without ceremony. The wine wasn't seemingly infused with Provence's rich herby underbrush known as *garrigue*, like Saint Cosme's Gigondas, which we would taste the next day, nor elegantly deep and mineral, like Montirius's Gigondas, which I would stumble across in the years ahead. But it was laden with hardscrabble Grenache fruit and cut with enough fiery tannin to make it a quintessential Gigondas. We couldn't ask for more.

The starters came. I can't remember what they were, but no matter; we consumed them with relish. The bread was replenished, the wine re-poured. The wind screamed outside but we had refuge inside, and the edge was taken off our appetites. The wine was wonderfully rustic, and the bird, we knew, would be fabulously rustic. Rusticity, Joe and I agreed, ruled.

Madame brought out our birds. She said these were the last two, and that we had chosen well. With a parting *bon appétit,* she disappeared into the kitchen. At first glance, the bird looked like roasted squab covered with a rich sauce. I saw a succulent breast and quickly carved off a piece. It was sublime, cooked *à point,* moist and gamy with flavor and complete with a pellet of birdshot. Birdshot! I couldn't even believe it. The thought crossed my mind that they must have inserted it in the kitchen for effect. I maneuvered the pellet around with my tongue and spit it out. "Look!" I said to Joe, opening my hand in the circle of candlelight.

He glanced over. He was unfazed. "Have you looked at what you're eating?" he asked, pointing down at his plate. I looked at my plate. My eyes adjusted to the darkness. First, I saw the fine needlelike talons of feet, curled

in death. They lay on either side of the dish, as if to frame
the bird. But it was the centerpiece that arrested my eye:
It was the face and head of the bird, curled neatly on top
of itself, its eyes burned out by heat, its little beak wide
open, and a few little tough quills of what were once feathers still sticking out of the back of its neck.

"This," Joe said, "is bona fide rustic."

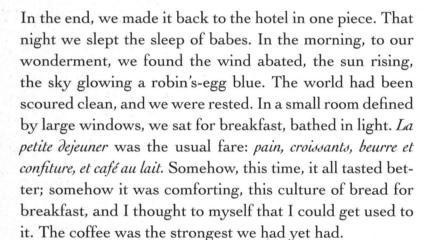

In the end, we made it back to the hotel in one piece. That
night we slept the sleep of babes. In the morning, to our
wonderment, we found the wind abated, the sun rising,
the sky glowing a robin's-egg blue. The world had been
scoured clean, and we were rested. In a small room defined
by large windows, we sat for breakfast, bathed in light. *La
petite dejeuner* was the usual fare: *pain, croissants, beurre et
confiture, et café au lait.* Somehow, this time, it all tasted better; somehow it was comforting, this culture of bread for
breakfast, and I thought to myself that I could get used to
it. The coffee was the strongest we had yet had.

We packed up, paid our bill, and loaded the trunk of
the car. My suitcase went on the left, Joe's on the right,
with the computer case and shoulder bag for wine snug
in between, as always — everything going into its assigned
place by rote now — and down went the hatch. In no hurry
to climb into the car, Joe stretched, raising his arms to the
sky. The parking lot was bare ground covered over with
shingle and bordered by olive trees. The leaves of those

trees were silver-hued in the bright light of morning. The hotel was a one-story affair with walls of white stucco and wooden-slatted shutters painted a pastel blue. There were flower troughs under the windows of the same blue, and in summer I imagined them filled with red-blossomed geraniums. It was a postcard of Provence.

"Royboy," Joe said, "I don't want to go back to my life."

I looked across the car at him. He wasn't just joking, that was evident. His life was a struggle. He had a frustrating job to return to and two young kids who didn't much like the fact that their parents' marriage had failed. I thought about my own life, and the idea of returning home to this new job without any experience of how to proceed, and without Dad to back me up, froze me and turned my stomach to stone. I glanced back at the hotel. "Maybe," I offered, "we could rob a bank and hole up in Châteauneuf."

Joe raised his eyebrows. He considered the idea. "*Les Robbers from the Galets Roulés,*" he said.

I smiled. He smiled. "It's a beautiful day," he said. "Let's go see this guy in Gigondas."

"All right," I said.

That afternoon we were scheduled to catch the fast train in Avignon to begin our way home. As we drove to our final appointment, I understood that I would have to return to France at least once within a year's time. Building, to say nothing of maintaining, a portfolio was anything but a one-shot deal. The road I was looking at was a long one.

"Joe," I said, "there's no way I'm going to learn enough French between now and my next trip. I've got too much else to concentrate on."

"When's your next trip?"

"Next spring or fall."

"You're right," he said.

"Thanks."

"Sorry."

The road snaked down off the plateau and crossed the autoroute to the plain, making a straight line among those flat vineyards, orchards, and fields. At the crossroads of small villages, thick russet-colored plane trees, closely cropped at their crowns, sprouted up from the pavement without any protective curb. The ones particularly close to the road were painted with white lines at eye level in hopes of warding off the aberrant driver. In France, if you ran into a tree, it seemed that there wasn't much recourse in terms of law. You chalked it up to your own dumb luck or dumb fault and went on.

"Think you'd be free to come along again?" I asked.

"I was just thinking about that," Joe said. "It might be a good idea."

We drove up the long hill to Gigondas, snug against its savage, teethlike limestone outcroppings known as the *Dentelles de Montmirail*. *Dents* is French for teeth, and cleverly, when I was first learning the language, I figured that I understood the meaning of *dentelles*. It turns out, however, that *dentelles* refers to lace, not to teeth. Evidently, some prominent citizen way back when looked upon those jagged stone fangs cresting Gigondas's verdant crown and perceived a delicate beauty.

The Montmirail range faces the vast Plein de Dieu, or Plain of God, which separates the Montmirails from the smaller, far gentler hills of Châteauneuf-du-Pape. In the old days this plain was patched with forest and meadows, and shepherds ran their flocks amid its open spaces. It was also the province of highwaymen, who gave the plain such a fearful reputation that citizens were always sure to give a prayer of thanks for safe passage at the end of their crossing. Thus was a name born.

Today the plain is covered in vines. These vines grow right up to the base of the moundlike hill leading up to Gigondas, and they continue up the mound's long flank, branching into lean, winding parcels to reach around the village and climb the steep ravines and hillsides that rise abruptly behind it. The softball-size stones of Châteauneuf were polished round by fast currents long ago and sit upon a dense layer of glacial and river deposits. The ground of Gigondas, by contrast, is marked by the chipped stone erosions coming off its limestone outcroppings, outcroppings that were thrust upward during a geological upheaval. As we began our drive up, we faced the three *terroirs* of the western Gigondas appellation: bottom slope (hot); mid-slope (warm); and top slope, or mountain elevations (cold).

Just before the village, we turned left and pulled into the driveway of Château de Saint Cosme ("comb").

Château is a relative term, this being Provence rather than Bordeaux. Saint Cosme is a tall, stately, eighteenth-century stone house with a couple outbuildings, one housing the winery, which is actually a series of buildings built half into a hillside, and another housing the office.

And there we met Louis Barruol. We found him in one of the winery buildings, in a room that opened to a kind of loading dock, and we walked up to the dock from the outside and watched as this lean little man with broad shoulders and a square forehead restlessly bent over a brand-new bottling machine above us. Bottling machines are intricate affairs. They have snaking conveyor belts to carry bottles along an assembly line that disinfects them, fills them with wine, pushes in corks, plops on decorative capsules, squeezes the capsules to mold to the bottle necks, slaps on labels, and carries the bottles to a way station to be boxed by human hands.

"Are you Roy?" the man asked, peering over the gleaming apparatus. I answered that I was. "Right," he said. He stood straight. "I've spent the morning messing with this machine. It's a super *bonne* machine, but it's Italian and all the instructions are in Italian." As an afterthought, he added, "*Putain.*"

The French curse aside, he spoke English with an English accent. That was disconcerting; he was French, after all. He came from one of those ancient French families that has been anchored for century after century after century in a little half-forgotten hilltop village with a fortified wall that had long since crumbled into ruin. I had read about this. Guys like him existed all over France. And they didn't have English accents.

"You would think," he went on, scowling at his new apparatus, "that they would at least write instructions in English. I learned English in England. I *know* English! *Putain!!* Bloody English, bloody Italians, bloody hell!" He paused. He looked down at us standing on the driveway. "Do you want to taste some wine?"

Before we could answer, he smiled at his own grandstanding. He waved us up the stairs. "Come on," he said. "We forget this machine. I have prepared a nice tasting for you."

Up we went to shake hands and be properly introduced. He took us on a quick tour of the place, and it became clear soon enough that the winery as such had been added to chamber by chamber over various epochs, and in the process had become something of a labyrinth. The primary structure followed the contour of the hillside, having dug chambers out of the stone and then expanding outward from those chambers. The centerpiece of the tour was the museum room, dedicated to winemaking. The Barruol family had been here since at least 1495; Louis was the fourteenth generation. The room was filled with artifacts from bygone eras: an old press, various tools, racks and racks of older vintages, fossils and ancient ceramics dug up from the vineyards, and Roman winemaking vats carved into the stone upon which Saint Cosme is built. There are two such vats, about the size of deep bathtubs, one above the other so these early winemakers could rack the wine from one vat to the other by gravity, a technique much touted these days for its gentleness compared to pumps. "Those Romans," Louis said, "what do we know that they didn't know?"

"Bottling machines?" Joe offered.

"That is true!" Louis agreed. "But I am not sure that is an improvement!"

He led us past contemporary vats built hard up against the stone to a small barrel room. A little white shaggy terrier came out of some nook and followed. He wasn't really white, not anymore, but he was a content little dog and he plopped himself down under a dangerously steep metal staircase next to Louis. That was his spot on the cement floor. Louis's spot was two feet away, under the stairs and between a wall and an upended barrel. It was here, with bottles of wine in a row on the floor behind him, and with a spit bucket, the latest glassware, and the bottle being tasted on the barrel in front of him, that Louis held court. This was where he conducted his tastings.

Joe leaned against one row of double-stacked barrels. I leaned against a parallel row. Louis stood behind his upended barrel. I opened my notebook to a fresh page. "*Putain!*" Louis roared. The dog raised an ear. Louis exited, racing up the steel staircase, disappearing. The staircase was a basic fire escape model that scaled the side of a vat at an extreme pitch (narrow room, tall vat), so much so that Joe and I marveled at the speed Louis climbed it. He disappeared for a moment, then came back down. He took the stairs sideways, one hand on the railing, another holding a bottle, and his legs worked like pistons to take him down even more nimbly than they took him up. Later, I would learn that Louis was an avid rugby player on the Vaison-la-Romaine team, and his heroes were the New Zealand All Blacks (so called because of their black jerseys, one of which hung on a wall in Louis's office and had, as care instructions on its tag, the bare-bones statement: THE ONLY CARE IS TO WIN). Still later on one of my visits Louis would claim that he quit his beloved sport when he discovered that he was no longer the fastest player on the Vaison team. He saw his ebbing speed as a sure sign that his day had come, and so, one was left to infer, he took his bow.

But in 1997 he was at the height of his physical prowess, and he displayed barely any shortness of breath upon resuming his station behind the barrel. "Sorry," he said, a little sheepishly. "I forgot the first wine."

The wine was his white Côtes du Rhône. Usually this kind of wine is simple and dull. The sunny south's strength is its red, not white. Louis poured the wine into three large crystal glasses. We had come a long way from old André Mussy's Burgundy snifter glasses. We each took a long-stemmed glass and swirled and sniffed; at once it was clear that this was no ordinary white Côtes du Rhône. Its aromas sprang forth, rich with bright scents of sun-drenched fruit. It was the kind of wine you wanted to smell several times before tasting. We did this without a word and then tilted the glasses back to take in the wine. Quietly, each of us let it run over our tongues time and again — Louis looking off in a corner; Joe looking down at that dog; me shutting my eyes—and the rich quality of mature fruit that we had smelled we now tasted. It was a big wine, even explosive, and vivaciously pure and clean.

Louis expelled the wine with a dexterous stream into the bucket. Joe bent over and blew out a big mouthful with a great splash. He stepped back, wiping his beard, nodding with excitement. "Buddy," he said, "you don't like shy wine, do you?"

Louis smiled, and nodded too by way of acknowledgment. "No," he replied, "I don't like shy wines." Then he paused, his expression turning serious, and asked, "But what do you mean, exactly?"

"I mean," Joe said, "you like expressive wines."

"Ah," said Louis, "that's true. That's true. But do you find this to be a good expression or a bad one?"

"Good," I answered. "Because this wine is refreshing." This hung in the air a moment, long enough for me to wonder if I had just stuck my foot in my mouth.

"I'm glad you said that," Louis said. "Because *that* is the challenge. Anyone can make a fat wine. That's easy! But what is a fat wine without freshness, without definition?" He looked at us. When we didn't answer, he stuck his butt out and went *tthhhiüüüüüüðð* with his tongue.

"Just a fart in the wind," Joe observed.

"Just a fart in the wind," Louis repeated. "And there is a lot of farting out there. Too much farting. Don't you agree? Right. So much for the starter wine. Let's taste the Condrieu. What do you say?"

"Okay," I said, with a smile.

"Okay," Joe echoed, with a wider smile.

"Okay," Louis affirmed, with a grin. He reached down, grabbed the bottle of Condrieu off the floor, and inserted the corkscrew. "But seriously," he added, "without definition, there is no elegance. Here in the south, elegance is what we go knocking at windmills for, and if we achieve it—if we capture elegance and marry it with ripeness— well then, we have won a victory."

As he pulled the cork, I pictured this powerful little man astride a donkey, corkscrew lance in hand: Don Louis Quixote lunging at a distant windmill to defeat the forces of evil and defend the virtues of Dulcinea, and in so doing gaining the holy grail of elegance. Now there was a worthy fight!

He poured the Condrieu. Condrieu, the home of Viognier, is a small appellation clinging to the steep hillsides just south of Lyon. Here in the 1960s Viognier very nearly passed away into extinction (at one point, according to the written record, only twenty-five acres of vines remained). Then it was rediscovered. It was quickly planted all over southern France, and indeed all over the world. But nowhere else does Viognier achieve such perfume coupled with such luscious body as in Condrieu. Condrieu, as Louis has said many a time, is truly a great *terroir*.

Louis's rendition wafted from our glasses in a plume of honeyed minerality. We bent over and became engulfed in the fragrance. I glanced at Joe: Nose in glass, he sniffed a great sniff, and at once the vision of him taking in the marvelous sea scent of scallops and mussels infused with

Pernod that bone-chilling evening in Sancerre came to my mind's eye. It was a fine memory, and I burst out laughing. Joe and Louis looked at me. "I'm sorry," I said, "I was just reminded of something, something that has nothing to do with wine, but actually has everything to do with wine, but anyway that's another story—this, Louis, *this* wine has extraordinary aromatics! If it tastes anything like it smells, then I'm sure I'm going to see God."

Louis's face lit up. "I hope so!" he said. "And be sure to tell me what he looks like!"

I raised my glass in salute and tasted the wine. We all did. The flavors were exotic, but teasing because like all things exotic they did not correspond to anything I really knew; they were not like any fruit that I could readily identify. Combinations of guava, papaya, and various melons went through my mind, all mixed up with honey and underpinned by zesty lees and delectable minerality. The texture and richness were as extraordinary as the aromatics.

After a minute of quiet slurping, I spit my mouthful into the bucket. I waited to see where the finish of the wine would take me, what it would say, what it would show. What I found was a talented man who could coax a great vineyard into singing its song, and that was a neat thing. That was a reason for living. I looked at Joe. Then I turned to Louis. "God," I told him happily, "is a beautiful feline creature."

"I knew it!" he exclaimed.

EPILOGUE

*I*n June of 2010 Helen and I drove down to the farm for a family meeting. My sister had taken the train to DC from New York, and she was in the car with us. Our other sister was flying in from Chicago with her husband. Joe was already on hand, having moved to the Shenandoah Valley from Seattle earlier in the decade to start a new career.

This was the third such meeting in as many years. They were Mom's idea, designed to manage the transition of property between the generations. She had this farm courtesy of Dad, who had led the charge to return east in retirement. He was there, but he didn't participate in the meetings; they occupied a different playing field now from his own. Instead, he presided over dinners, standing to issue the refrain of what a joy it was to be in the bosom of the family (he had never lost his charm), and then he sat, his book next to his dinner plate.

He read histories and biographies, and the newspaper, endlessly and quietly. What was retained or comprehended was not really clear to us. Every so often, however, the newspaper would inspire a letter. These were usually addressed to someone important—the president or vice president or a senator or the head of the Nuclear Regulatory Agency—outlining some harebrained idea (shoot off radioactive waste to the moon!) or filled with an abridged version of his life story. Invariably, he signed off as Dr. Robert Cloud, or, sometimes, if he was in a particularly benevolent mood, Dr. Bob (he did, after all, have a doctorate in mechanical engineering).

Not all of his routines were quiet, though. One was to get on the lawn tractor each morning and drive up the hill to Steve's house, where he could bum a smoke and have a cup of coffee. He had smoked as a young man and those memories were the live ones. Afterward, he would climb back on the little tractor and come home. He had cleverly realized early on that he could go a lot faster if he just cut the engine and coasted down the hill. The bottom leveled out shortly before our driveway, and he had to fire up the engine to finish the final leg home. But on the way down he was able to gather a good amount of speed, and at least once he hit a bump at the bottom of the hill just right, causing Steve's grandson to burst into the kitchen to announce, "*Holy cow, Dr. Cloud just caught air!*"

Mom had long since given up trying to stop him. Doing so was all but impossible, and the fact is the lawn tractor and cigarettes were among the few joys and manifestations of independence left in his life. Fortunately, unlike a road bike, the tractor had four wheels rather than two, and a low center of gravity.

For one of the dinners during this reunion, Joe had supplied the meat for a big daube that Mom made days in advance. Joe had gone into the meat business. For a long time he had wanted to return to a rural life (we grew up on a farm as children), and after his daughter went off to college, he left Seattle and his job and invested in an abattoir in the valley with a local farmer of some repute in the food movement. Nowadays, the company, T&E Meats, slaughters animals for small farms in the area that wouldn't otherwise have a place to process their livestock. It was, admittedly, a radical departure from what Joe had been doing, but he likes working with farmers. He's remarried and lives up the hill next to Steve.

Joe did return with me to France the following year after that first trip. But he never managed to get away again, and from then on I dealt with France on my own. In 2002 the winery that owned the importing company decided that it wanted out of the importing business. I only had two options: shut down the business or try to buy it. In the end, this wasn't a hard decision, for I had already invested too much of myself in the company to let it go. Funds were found, debt secured, and an agreement was reached with the winery. I renamed the business Vintage '59 Imports, an iconic vintage in France and my birth year.

It was late in the afternoon when Helen and I drove up the driveway of the farm. Joe came out of the house, followed by Mom and Dad, to walk the long brick path to the garage. Dad held onto Mom's arm because his own walking was not the steadiest. Balance was one of the things he had lost in the accident. In the garage, he got on his lawn tractor. There was a little wagon attached to it now. He drove over next to the car and turned the engine off so that he might hear.

"HEY, HOW'S IT GOING, DAD?" my sister screamed. She had to scream; he had become all but deaf.

He smiled broadly. "Baby," he said, "it's good to see you. Now put your bag in here."

She dropped her knapsack in the wagon, and Joe and I loaded in other bags and suitcases for him to take to the house. We waited for him to turn the key and pull away, but he had spied the case of wine in the trunk of my car.

"What's that?" he asked.

"Wine," I admitted, knowing if I put the case in his wagon that I might never see it again.

"Put it in the wagon," he said.

"I wouldn't want to tempt you into hiding it under the porch," I said. Wine, like cigarettes, was a weakness for him.

"*What?*" he asked, his face scrunched in an exaggerated frown.

"IT'S WHITE WINE," I hollered, and pulled out a bottle to prove it. It was a bottle of Merlin-Cherrier's 2007 Sancerre Chêne Marchand. "This may be the best one Thierry's ever made," I said under my breath to Joe.

"All right!" Joe said. "We'll have to find some scallops!"

"White wine?" Dad said.

"YES! SORRY!"

Normally, for him, a wine's first duty was to be red. But this time his face blissfully relaxed, and he shrugged with equanimity. "Sonny," he said, and smiled, "if it's good wine, I would like to try it."

That broke my defenses as easily as matchsticks. "IT'S GOOD, DAD," I said. "IT REALLY IS."

"Well then," he replied magnanimously, "our path lies clear before us."

ACKNOWLEDGMENTS

My thanks to Judith Harway for her time and acute perceptions; to my agent Farley Chase for fighting the good fight; and to my editor Holly Rubino and her colleagues, all of whom lent a fine hand in the final stage.

My special thanks to Jacques Schlumberger and Jerry Craven, who made it possible.

ABOUT THE AUTHOR

Roy Cloud is the president of Vintage '59 Imports. He lives in Washington DC, with his wife, Helen Michael, and Zeus and Hercules (the Greek guys are their cats).